RISKING

Sometimes it seems to me that in this absurdly random life there is some inherent justice in the outcome of personal relationships. In the long run, we get no more than we have been willing to risk giving.

LOVE

Love is more than simply being open to experiencing the anguish of another person's suffering. It is the willingness to live with the helpless knowing that we can do nothing to save the other from his pain.

THE DEPENDENT DISCIPLE

While seeking to be taught the Truth the disciple learns only that there is nothing that anyone else can teach him . . . *The secret is that there is no secret*.

IF YOU MEET THE BUDDHA ON THE ROAD, KILL HIM!

If You Meet The Buddha on the Road, Kill Him!

THE PILGRIMAGE OF PSYCHOTHERAPY PATIENTS

Sheldon B. Kopp

BANTAM BOOKS

NEW YORK · TORONTO · LONDON · SYDNEY · AUCKLAND

*This edition contains the complete text
of the original hardcover edition.*
NOT ONE WORD HAS BEEN OMITTED.

IF YOU MEET THE BUDDHA ON THE ROAD, KILL HIM!
*A Bantam Book / published by arrangement with
Science and Behavior Books, Inc.*

PRINTING HISTORY
Science and Behavior edition published December 1972
Bantam edition / May 1976
16 printings through August 1988

*For information address: Science and Behavior Books, Inc.,
P.O. Box 60519, Palo Alto, Calif. 94306.*

ISBN 0-553-27832-0

Published simultaneously in the United States and Canada

Bantam Books are published by Bantam Books, a division of
Bantam Doubleday Dell Publishing Group, Inc. Its trademark,
consisting of the words "Bantam Books" and the portrayal of
a rooster, is Registered in U.S. Patent and Trademark Office
and in other countries. Marca Registrada. Bantam Books,
666 Fifth Avenue, New York, New York 10103.

PRINTED IN THE UNITED STATES OF AMERICA

KR   25 24 23 22 21 20 19 18 17

For my dead parents, whom I often miss:

My Mother whose strength and ferocity nurtured me, almost did me in, and taught me how to survive.

And my Father whose gentleness and passivity showed me how to love, let me down often, and freed me to find my own way.

Acknowledgments

The author gratefully acknowledges the permission granted by publishers and copyright holders to quote from the following works:

The I Ching: Or Book of Changes translated by Richard Wilhelm, rendered into English by Cary F. Baynes, Bollingen Series XIX; copyright 1950 and 1967 by Bollingen Foundation; reprinted by permission of Princeton University Press and Routledge & Kegan Paul, Ltd. *Tao Tê Ching* by Lao Tzu, translated by D. C. Lau; copyright 1963 by Penguin Books, Ltd. *The Gates of the Forest* by Elie Wiesel, translated by Frances Frenaye; copyright 1966 by Holt, Rinehart and Winston, Inc.; reprinted by permission of Holt, Rinehart and Winston, Inc., and George Borchardt, Inc. *The Gilgamesh Epic and Old Testament Parallels,* edited by A. Heidel; copyright 1946 and 1949 by Chicago University Press. *Siddhartha* by Hermann Hesse, translated by Hilda Rosner; copyright 1951 by New Directions Publishing Corp.

The Canterbury Tales by Geoffrey Chaucer, translated by Nevill Coghill; copyright 1951, 1958, and 1960 by Nevill Coghill; reprinted by permission of Penguin Books, Ltd. *The Pilgrim's Progress* by John Bunyan, edited by Roger Sharrock; copyright 1965 by Penguin Books, Inc. *Heart of Darkness* by Joseph Conrad; copyright 1960 by J. M. Dent & Sons, Ltd. *Between Man and Man* by Martin Buber; copyright 1947 by Routledge & Kegan Paul, Ltd.; reprinted with permission of The Macmillan Company. *Howl and Other*

Poems by Allen Ginsburg; copyright 1956 and 1959 by Allen Ginsburg; reprinted by permission of City Lights Books. *The Way and Its Power* by Arthur Waley, published by George Allen & Unwin, Ltd. From the book *The Way of the Sufi* by Indries Shah; copyright 1968 by Indries Shah; published in a paperback edition by E. P. Dutton & Co., Inc., and used with their permission.

The author would also like to thank the following publishers for allowing him to reprint or adapt material from the following works:

Voices, "A Mother's Love," Spring 1966; "Some for Him and Some for Me," Winter 1967; "An Eschatological Laundry List," Fall 1970; "Dream Two: Nothing Ever Really Changes," Fall 1971. *Psychological Perspectives*, "The Discontented Disciple," Spring 1972.

I am grateful for the help and encouragement along the way which was tendered by three friends whose heads and hearts I trust: Don Lathrop, Gary Price and Toby Tate.

Contents

If You Meet
The Buddha
On the Road,
Kill Him!

Part One: Take from No Man His Song

1. Pilgrims and Disciples

> DIFFICULTY AT THE BEGINNING works supreme
>   success.
> Furthering through perseverance.
> Nothing should be undertaken
> It furthers one to appoint helpers.
> *I Ching*[1]

In every age, men have set out on pilgrimages, on spiritual journeys, on personal quests. Driven by pain, drawn by longing, lifted by hope, singly and in groups they come in search of relief, enlightenment, peace, power, joy or they know not what. Wishing to learn, and confusing being taught with learning, they often seek out helpers, healers, and guides, spiritual teachers whose disciples they would become.

The emotionally troubled man of today, the contemporary pilgrim, wants to be the disciple of the psychotherapist. If he does seek the guidance of such a contemporary guru, he will find himself beginning on a latter-day spiritual pilgrimage of his own.

This should not surprise us. Crises marked by anxiety, doubt, and despair have always been those periods of personal unrest that occur at the times when a man is sufficiently unsettled to have an opportunity for personal growth. We must always see our own feelings of uneasiness as being our chance for "making the growth choice rather than the fear choice."[2]

So, too, the patient's *longing* for growth is the central force of his pilgrimage.

The psychotherapist needs only to be aware of this force, in his patient, and to keep it within his vision.

Then he may enjoy his work, and need never bog down in boredom. His task is simply to watch, as the person in front of him wrestles with well-nigh paralyzing conflict, for the emergence of what he knows is there: man's inherent longing for relatedness and for meaning. The therapist is an observer and a catalyst. He has no power to "cure" the patient, for cure is entirely out of his hands. He can add nothing to the patient's inherent capacity to get well, and whenever he tries to do so he meets stubborn resistance which slows up the progress of treatment. The patient is already fully equipped for getting well. . . . Since he [the therapist] is not "responsible" for the cure, he is free to enjoy the spectacle of it taking place.[3]

Of course, like everyone else (including the therapist), the patient is too often inclined to act out of fear, rather than out of his longing for growth. If not, pilgrimages would always begin out of an overflow of joy, rather than (as is more often the case) being conceived in pain and turmoil. People seek the guidance of a psychotherapist when their usual, self-limited, risk-avoiding ways of operating are not paying off, when there is distress and disruption in their lives. Otherwise, we are all too ready to live with the familiar, so long as it seems to work, no matter how colorless the rewards.

And so, it is not astonishing that, though the patient enters therapy insisting that he wants to change, more often than not, what he really wants is to remain the same and to get the therapist to make him feel better. His goal is to become a more effective neurotic, so that he may have what he wants without risking getting into anything new. He prefers the security of known misery to the misery of unfamiliar insecurity.

Given this all too human failing, the beginning pilgrim-patient may approach the therapist like a small child going to a good parent whom he insists must take care of him. It is as if he comes to the office saying, "My world is broken, and you have to fix it."

Because of this, my only goals as I begin the work are to take care of myself and to have fun. The patient must provide the motive power of our interaction. It is as if I stand in the doorway of my office, waiting. The patient enters and makes a lunge at me, a desperate attempt to pull me into the fantasy of taking care of him. I step aside. The patient falls to the floor, disappointed and bewildered. Now he has a chance to get up and to try something new. If I am sufficiently skillful at this psychotherapeutic judo, and if he is sufficiently courageous and persistent, he may learn to become curious about himself, to come to know me as I am, and to begin to work out his own problems. He may transform his stubbornness into purposeful determination, his bid for safety into a reaching out for adventure.

You may then ask, "Of what sustained value is the presence of the therapist to such a seeker?" He can be useful in many ways. The therapist, first of all, provides another struggling human being to be encountered by the then self-centered patient, who can see no other problems than his own. The therapist can interpret, advise, provide the emotional acceptance and support that nurtures personal growth, and above all, he can listen. I do not mean that he can simply hear the other, but that he will *listen* actively and purposefully, responding with the instrument of his trade, that is, with the personal vulnerability of his own trembling self. This listening is that which will facilitate the patient's telling of his tale, the telling that can set him free.

The therapist provides a "dreamlike atmosphere . . . , and in it . . . [the patient] has nothing to rely upon except . . . [his] own so fallible subjective judgment."[4] I have pirated this description. It was written by Carl Jung to describe the usefulness of the *I Ching*, the three-thousand-year-old Chinese *Book of Changes*, some lines from which I have used to begin this chapter.

At first, the patient tries to use the therapist, as many over the centuries have tried to use the *I Ching*, the oldest book of divination. The *Book of Changes* is made up of images from the mythology and social and religious institutions of the time of its origin. Orientals have too often searched these images for oracular guidance, just as some Christians have opened the Bible to verses picked at random in hope of getting specific advice about how to solve problems. So, too, the psychotherapy patient may begin by trying to get the therapist to tell him what he is to do to be happy and how he is to live without being fully responsible for his own life.

However, the *I Ching*, the Holy Bible, the contemporary psychotherapist and other gurus, all are poor oracles. They are instead far more significant as wellsprings of wisdom about the ambiguity, the insolubility, and the inevitability of the human situation. Their value lies just in their offering imagery that is fixed without being stereotyped, images "to meditate upon, and to discover one's identity in."[5] To these wellsprings, the seeker must bring himself, and then listen for the echo returned by the books of wisdom or by his guru. Coming to knowledge of the self is insisted upon throughout the pilgrimage. The helper provides "one long admonition to careful scrutiny of one's own character, attitude, and motives."[6]

The seeker comes in hope of finding something definite, something permanent, something unchanging upon which to depend. He is offered instead the reflection that life is just what it seems to be, a changing, ambiguous, ephemeral mixed bag. It may often be discouraging, but it is ultimately worth it, because that's all there is. The pilgrim-patient wants a definite way of living, and is shown that:

> The way that can be spoken of
> Is not the constant way;
> The name that can be named
> Is not the constant name.[7]

He may only get to keep that which he is willing to let go of. The cool water of the running stream may be scooped up with open, overflowing palms. It cannot be *grasped* up to the mouth with clenching fists, no matter what thirst motivates our desperate grab.

Starting out as he does in the urgency of his mission, it is difficult for the pilgrim to learn this patient yielding. This is to be seen in the old Zen story of the three young pupils whose Master instructs them that they must spend a time in complete silence if they are to be enlightened. "Remember, not a word from any of you," he admonishes. Immediately, the first pupil says, "I shall not speak at all." "How stupid you are," says the second. "Why did you talk?" "I am the only one who has not spoken," concludes the third pupil.[8]

The pilgrim, whether psychotherapy patient or earlier wayfarer, is at war with himself, in a struggle with his own nature. All of the truly important battles are waged within the self. It is as if we are all tempted to view ourselves as men on horseback.[9] The horse represents a lusty animal-way of living, untrammeled by reason, unguided by purpose. The rider represents independent, impartial thought, a sort of pure cold intelligence. Too often the pilgrim lives as though his goal is to become the horseman who would break the horse's spirit so that he can control him, so that he may ride safely and comfortably wherever he wishes to go. If he does not wish to struggle for discipline, it is because he believes that his only options will be either to live the lusty, undirected life of the riderless horse, or to tread the detached, unadventuresome way of the horseless rider. If neither of these, then he must be the rider struggling to gain control of his rebellious mount. He does not see that there will be no struggle, once he recognizes himself as a *centaur*.

If he ever achieves his true nature, gets beyond the point of struggle, he may wonder why the therapist-guru did not tell him at once the simple truths that would have made him free. But as a therapist, I know that though the patient learns, I do not teach. Furthermore, what is to be learned is too elusively simple to be grasped without *struggle, surrender,* and *experiencing* of how it is. As one Zen Master said to his now-enlightened pupil:

> If I did not make you fight in every way possible in order to find the meaning [of Zen] and lead you finally to a state of non-fighting and of no-effort from which you can see with your own eyes, I am sure that you would lose every chance of discovering yourself.[10]

This search for enlightenment, pursued in a secular context by today's psychotherapy patient, has in the past been cast in religious terms. Whatever the metaphors in which the pilgrim experiences his quest, any trip involving a search for spiritual meaning is an allegorical journey through life, a journey that can renew and enrich the quality of the rest of the pilgrim's daily living. The pilgrim, "strengthened by desire and hope, burdened with anxiety and fear, beset by temptations and guarded by spiritual powers, pursues his way along the Path of Life, seeking ever 'a better country.'"[11]

The early history of the pilgrimage is a variegated story of journeys made for reasons both sacred and profane to those holy places where a god resides, or where a prophet has appeared, or where a hero has been martyred. Pilgrimages were made by pagan Greeks and by the inhabitants of the ancient sites of other early Mediterranean civilizations, by orientals, Egyptians, Jews, and Christians.

The primitive Aborigines of Australia also make ceremonial trips to holy places, places whose origin their myths describe:

> The two Djanggau Sisters came across the water . . . traveling on the path of the rising sun from an island away to the northeast. They made the first people. They made the water holes and *the sacred ritual sites.*
>
> At first the sisters possessed all the most secret sacred objects, the most sacred rites. Men had nothing. And so men stole them. But the sisters, said, "Oh,

let them keep those things. Now men can do this work, looking after those things for everybody."[12]

And to this day, Aboriginal men still make pilgrimages to the sacred ritual sites to look after things.

In the Orient, pilgrimages have long been, and still are, common ways of fulfilling spiritual vows. Buddha himself has been called "the Great Pilgrim."[13] In Islam, Mohammed, the Prophet of Allah, proclaimed it the duty of every Muslim to visit Mecca at least once in his lifetime. As a result, Mecca, the birthplace of Mohammed, has become the center of religious life of the Muslim world.

Christians, too, have long found it rewarding to make pilgrimages. From the close of the eleventh century on, they undertook several great crusading expeditions. Taking up the Cross and forsaking their homes, thousands ventured out for the love of God, or for their own material gain. They made the far journey to the places in which the Savior is said to have walked. Whatever their motives, they went in the company of other seekers; they found community with others as they exchanged tales, made themselves known to one another, and examined the meaning of their lives.

Even before (as well as after) the Crusades, many were used to the familiar habit of journeying to the shrines of local saints. Some were sick and sought a cure. Others, now recovered, went to fulfill a vow of gratitude. Many went to expiate their sins, as a communal expression of penances. Some even went as a form of social protest, to honor a dissident hero. "To make a saint of a rebel was the most energetic means of protesting against the king."[14]

Whatever the initial motives, such a journey often gave the pilgrims new perspective on the meaning of their lives, made them "converts to better lives, [at least] for a time."[15] The metaphor of his journey is a *bridge,* and as the pilgrim crosses it, "a fiend clutches at him from behind; and Death awaits him at the farther end."[16] But there are companions and helpers along the

way as well. One pilgrim may help another as when a
blind man carries one who is lame upon his back, so
that together they may make a pilgrimage that neither
could make alone.

By acts of devotion, the crossing of this bridge may
be undertaken. But the call to the difficult life of pilgrimage may be ignored or denied. Christ admonishes:

> Enter ye in at the strait gate: for wide *is* the gate, and
> broad *is* the way, that leadeth to destruction, and
> many there be which go in thereat:
>   Because strait *is* the gate, and narrow *is* the way
> which leadeth unto life, and few there be that find it.[17]

And a journey may be a flight, rather than a search.
James Joyce, the Irish expatriate, went to find his place
in Paris, and spent the rest of his life in exile there,
writing about life in Dublin, the home from which he
had escaped. Someone once suggested that his God-
term should have been a *pier,* rather than the *bridge* of
pilgrimages, for a pier is a bridge that goes nowhere.

Search we must. Each man must set out to cross his
bridge. The important thing is to begin. "A journey of
a thousand miles starts from beneath one's feet."[18] But,
remember, setting out does not by itself guarantee success. There is beginning, but there is also perserving,
that is, beginning again and again and again. You are
well advised to set out with a *professional pilgrim as a
guide.* Such men of lifelong calling (or penace) are
easily recognizable, "adorned with many tokens, the
witness of many wonders, the hero of many adventures."[19]

And remember, too, you can stay at home, safe in
the familiar illusion of certainty. Do not set out without realizing that "the way is not without danger.
Everything good is costly, and the development of the
personality is one of the most costly of all things."[20]
It will cost you your innocence, your illusions, your
certainty.

2. The Healing Metaphors of the Guru

> He finds a comrade,
> Now he beats the drum, now he stops.
> Now he sobs, now he sings.[1]
> *I Ching*

Some men undertake their pilgrimages in solitude, others in the company of other seekers. Even those who set out alone may find helpful companions who join them along the way. But for most of us, at the troubled time at which we set out on the search for the meaning of our lives, it seems wise to turn to a helper, a healer, or a guide who can show us the way (or at least can turn us away from the dead-end paths we usually walk). "Priests and magicians are used in great number."[2]

Such a spiritual guide is sometimes called a *Guru*. This special sort of teacher helps others through the rites of initiation and transition by seeming to introduce his disciples to the new experiences of higher levels of spiritual understanding. In reality, what he offers them is guidance toward accepting their imperfect, finite existence in an ambiguous and ultimately unmanageable world. Gurus may at first appear to be "the ideal bearers of final truths, but [in reality, they are] simply . . . the *most extraordinarily human* members of the community."[3] Even the contemporary Western guru, the psychotherapist, can only be of help to that extent to which he is a fellow-pilgrim.

The guru will appear in different forms. He may wear the garb of a simple teacher or an itinerate healer. Or he may come upon the scene with the dramatic force of a prophet, a sage, or even a wizard, depending upon the time and place of his appearance. He will fit the cultural expectations, even though he may be responded to as much with distrust and fear as with confidence and respect.

Both the awe that he commands and the distress that he engenders are, in part, responses to his radical, even charismatic, strangeness to all rules and traditions. Arising in a revolutionary context, he sets himself against both the traditional authority of patriarchal domination and the bureaucratic legalistic defining of power. Unintimidated by cultural expectations, he is his own man, piercing the group's conventional wisdom and overturning the usual ways of understanding the meaning of life.

His impact comes in part from his speaking the forgotten language of prophecy, the poetic language of the myth and of the dream. "If the myth is the outer expression of the human condition's basic struggles, joys, and ambiguities, then the dream is its inner voice."[4] The guru teaches indirectly, not by way of dogma and lecture, but by means of parable and metaphor.

Instruction by metaphor does not depend primarily on rationally determined logical thinking nor on empirically objective checking of perceptual data. Instead, knowing metaphorically implies grasping a situation intuitively, in its many interplays of multiple meanings, from the concrete to the symbolic. In this way, as the Sufies demonstrate with their Teaching-Stories, these inner dimensions make the parable capable of revealing more and more levels of meaning, depending on the disciple's level of readiness to understand. By way of example, here is the Sufi Teaching-Story of the Water-Melon Hunter:

Once upon a time, there was a man who strayed from his own country into the world known as the Land of Fools. He soon saw a number of people flying in terror from a field where they had been trying to reap wheat.

"There is a monster in that field," they told him. He looked, and saw that it was a water-melon.

He offered to kill the "monster" for them. When he had cut the melon from its stalk, he took a slice and began to eat it. The people became even more terrified of him than they had been of the melon. They drove him away with pitchforks, crying, "He will kill us next, unless we get rid of him."

It so happened that at another time another man also strayed into the Land of Fools, and the same thing started to happen to him. But, instead of offering to help them with the "monster," he agreed with them that it must be dangerous, and by tiptoeing away from it with them he gained their confidence. He spent a long time with them in their houses until he could teach them, little by little, the basic facts which would enable them not only to lose their fear of melons, but even to cultivate them themselves.[5]

The Truth does *not* make people free. Facts do *not* change attitudes. If the guru is dogmatic, all that he evokes in his pilgrim/disciples is their stubbornly resistant insistence on clinging to those unfortunate beliefs that at least provide the security of known misery, rather than openness to the risk of the unknown or the untried. That is why that Renaissance Magus, Paracelsus, warned that the guru should avoid simply revealing "the naked truth. He should use images, allegories, figures, wondrous speech, or other hidden, roundabout ways."[6]

The earliest form in which the guru appeared was that of the shaman, who arose in the hunting and gathering societies of the paleolithic era (and among their contemporary Eskimo and Indian progeny). Before the advent of God and His priests in the more stable agricultural societies of the neolithic era, the shaman acted as spiritual leader to the nomadic, Stone-Age hunting band.

Such a guru starts out on his own tortured pilgrimage as a deeply troubled, misfit youth. In mastering his personal afflictions, he gradually comes to the position of being able to help others on their spiritual trips. Unlike the later priests who were ceremonially trained in ritual acts and verbatim incantations, the shaman has been inspired by the visions that arise during his own pilgrimage. The power of his growing self-awareness and the spontaneity of his improvisations fit the hunters' needs for daring and imagination (just as the priests' ritual intonements and predetermined social proscriptions fit the planters' needs for stability, achieved by the sacrifice of the individual to the greater good of the group).

The source of the shaman's moving inner vision is a journey deep into the self. Usually in a trance-like state, he experiences the struggle within his own soul as an encounter with the spirit world. In the religion, myths, and literature of every culture, the personal motives and conflicts that men would disown are represented by gods and ghosts, by spirits and visions. A young Eskimo neophyte shaman tells of his own transformation experience while out on the pilgrimage of a lonely wilderness vigil:

> I soon became melancholy. I would sometimes fall to weeping and feeling unhappy without knowing why. Then for no reason all would suddenly be changed, and I felt a great, inexplicable joy, a joy so powerful that I could not restrain it, but had to break into song, a mighty song, with room for only one word: joy, joy! And I had to use the full strength of my voice. And then in the midst of such a fit of mysterious and overwhelming delight, I became a shaman, not knowing myself how it came about. But I was a shaman. I could see and hear in a totally different way. I had gained my enlightenment, the shaman's light of brain and body, and this in such a manner that it was not only I who could see through the darkness of life, but the same bright light also shone out from me, imperceptible to human beings but visible to all spirits of earth and sky and sea, and these now came to me to become my helping spirits.[7]

After his pilgrimage, the shaman then returns to the community of his tribe, "reborn" by way of his self-healing process. Now he is able to liberate the ordinary hunters of the band by revealing to each of them his own personally enlightening inner vision.

The shaman can also bring spiritual calm and confidence to a troubled tribe by helping them to work out the merited misfortunes that have befallen them. He will usually go into a trance at such times, his helping spirits speaking through his mouth in those poetically cryptic ways in which spirits (and gurus) speak. They ask the troubled ones what is causing the unhappiness. The power of the shaman's personal presence leads the troubled person to acknowledge that his thoughts have been bad, and his actions evil. The helping spirits of the shaman then make veiled references that evoke the whole story.

For example, to a woman who has caused "bad blood" among the men by her seeming infidelity, the spirits may say: "I see a gleaming object, broken in your lower body." With the encouragement of the communal audience, the sufferer believes that she has been seen through, purges herself with an outpouring of confession of her misdeeds, and then talks out and settles the troubles between herself and other members of the tribe.

This purging brings peace to the tribe through constructive human interaction mediated by the inspiring power of the shaman's confidence in his own inner vision, and by the metaphorical evocation of the troubled seeker's own tale.

Another powerful example of the guru who instructs by metaphor may be found in the Zaddik, the spiritual leader of the Hasidim. The Hasidic phenomenon was "a Jewish mystical movement of the eighteenth and nineteenth centuries, a movement which brought a charm, a vitality, and a personal relevance that touched and renewed the lives of a despairing people."[8]

Devastated by Cossack oppression, the hope-starved

Jewish people had turned in vain desperation to the false messiahs who arose, and to the cultist esotericism of the masters of the Kabbalistic mysteries. They struggled to retain their faith in the covenant with God, the faith that their suffering had meaning. They found themselves fooled, betrayed, lost in a spiritual desert, and unable to understand the mysterious prophecies of the Kabbalists in which they had hoped to be able to believe.

It was in response to this desperate search for guidance that the Baal Shem-Tov, the first Zaddik, appeared. No longer would men have to depend on the magical authority of the priestly keepers of incomprehensible secret truths. Instead, this new guru promised that truth would be open to all men, that each would be able to renew his faith by joining the Zaddik on a personal pilgrimage. This guru would acknowledge his own human fallibility, yet trust his feelings, and expect a like commitment from those who would seek his guidance. They would no longer be bewildered pilgrims standing like children before the gates of the temple. The meanings which they sought would be accessible to all. No longer would there be a distinction between the sacred and the profane. Everyday life would be hallowed, and each man would be responsible for that bit of existence that God had entrusted to his care.

The guru of Hasidism would join the other pilgrims in their search, rather than offering them the authoritarian teachings of the high priest or wizard. One such Zaddik describes his leadership by likening his Hasidic pilgrims to a band of wanderers who have become lost in a deep, dark forest. They chance upon their guru, who has been lost even longer. Unaware of his helplessness, they ask him to show them the way out of the woods. He can only answer: "That I cannot do. But I can point out the ways that lead further into the thicket, and after that let us try to find the way together."[9]

Like the shaman, the Zaddik instructs by metaphor, by indirection, not by teaching the pilgrims to be more like him, but to be more like themselves. Rather than offer dogma to his followers, he offered himself. He was the teaching. His trembling before God inspired faith, and his risking being foolish gave the Hasidim the daring to be themselves. His stories instructed each pilgrim by way of what the seeker brought to it, rather than by laying down instructions on how to live.

So it was that when the Hasidic pilgrims vied for who among them had endured the most suffering who was most entitled to complain, the Zaddik told them the story of the Sorrow Tree. On the Day of Judgment, each person will be allowed to hang all of his unhappiness on a branch of the great Tree of Sorrows. After each person has found a limb from which his own miseries may dangle, they may all walk slowly around the tree. Each is to search for a set of sufferings that he would prefer to those he has hung on the tree. In the end, each man freely chooses to reclaim his own personal set of sorrows rather than those of another. Each man leaves the tree wiser than when he came.

The metaphorical teachings of the Hasidic guru sometimes took the form of his own personality being a substitute for dogma, of the pilgrim's relationship with him being the vehicle for salvation. Whatever the Zaddik was doing at any given moment was what mattered most to him, and he did it with his whole soul. Thus it was that his followers would come to him, not to be taught great truths, "but to watch him tie his bootlaces."[10]

As a final example of the guru who instructs by metaphor so that his disciples may learn what they already know, let us consider the Zen Master. The original Buddhist teachings first appeared in Southern India where they helped to free men from the imprisoning Hindu social caste system and the Yoga emphasis on control of mind and body. As the teachings were passed northward through China, they allowed men to see through the tradition-bound social conventions that held them fast. And then in Japan, the spirit of Zen imbued the Japanese penchant for ceremonial elegance with an absurdity that undid its own restrictions.

A favorite method of Zen guidance is the Koan ex-

ercise. The disciple is given a problem on which to
meditate, a problem that is insoluble by conventional
or intellectual means. With it the Zen pilgrim must
struggle until either he *gives up* in despair or he *gives
in* and is enlightened. A classical example is for the
master to direct him to concentrate on "the sound of
one hand clapping."

Such conundrums are often offered in response to the
young monk's demands for clarification. Ironically, it is
these very demands with which he confounds himself.
So it is that when he asks: "How can I ever get emanci-
pated?" the Zen Master may answer: "Who has ever
put you in bondage?"[11] Or, consider this exchange:

> A monk asked: What is the meaning of the First Patri-
>   archs' coming from the West?
> Master: Ask the post over there.
> Monk: I do not understand you.
> Master: I do not either, any more than you.[12]

Only by such indirection can the Master lead the
pilgrim to turn back to the here-and-now moments of
his everyday life, to learn that there is no truth that is
not already apparent to everyone. This sense of im-
mediacy without struggle comes across in the sad/
lovely parable of the Zen Master who, while out walking one day, is confronted by a ferocious, man-eating
tiger. He backs away from the animal, only to find that
he is trapped at the edge of a high cliff. The tiger pursues the Master whose only hope of escape is to suspend
himself over the abyss by holding on to a frail vine
that grows at its edge. Above is the tiger who would
devour him. Below is the certain death of a long fall
onto the jagged rocks. The slender vine begins to give
way, and death is imminent. Just then the precariously
suspended Zen Master notices a lovely ripe wild strawberry growing along the cliff's edge. He plucks the suc-
culent berry and pops it into his mouth. He is heard to
say: "This lovely strawberry, how sweet it tastes."

By speaking to him in metaphor, the guru turns the

pilgrim in upon himself. He offers the seeker only what he already possesses, taking from him that which he never had. What the guru knows that the seeker does not is that *we are all pilgrims*. There is no master, and there is no student. At its worst, the fundamental humanity of the guru may be expressed in his inevitable corruptibility. The grace of the guru and the disciples who take his place are subject to the same eventual decay that is the other face of all human forms of growth. The charisma of the guru may become as self-serving as the very Establishment against which it arose, as it is routinized by efforts to sustain its power. The arrogance of the guru may tempt him to self-elevation, or he may be done in by his followers' needs to make more of themselves through his apotheosis. Empty ritualistic parodies may eventually be all that are left of teachings that were once spontaneous and alive. The reification of his metaphors by those who take his place may lead to the hollow appearance of continuity, without the original life-giving substance of inspired teaching.

The teaching mission of the guru is an attempt to free his followers from him. His metaphors and parables make it necessary for the pilgrims who would be disciples to turn to their own imaginations in the search for meaning in their lives. The guru instructs the pilgrims in the tradition of breaking with tradition, in losing themselves so that they may find themselves.

3. Disclosing the Self

Contemplation of my life
Decides the choice
Between advance and retreat.[1]
Hidden dragon. Do not act.[2]
I Ching

The guru instructs by metaphor and parable, but the pilgrim learns through the telling of his own tale. Each man's identity is an emergent of the myths, rituals, and corporate legends of his culture, compounded with the epic of his own personal history. In either case, it is the compelling power of the storytelling that distinguishes men from beasts. The paradoxical interstice of power and vulnerability, which makes a man most human, rests on his knowing who he is right now, because he can remember who he has been, and because he knows who he hopes to become. All this comes of the wonder of his being able to tell his tale.

When the great Rabbi Israel Baal Shem-Tov saw misfortune threatening the Jews it was his custom to go into a certain part of the forest to meditate. There he would light a fire, say a special prayer, and the miracle would be accomplished and the misfortune averted.

Later, when his disciple, the celebrated Magid of Mezritch, had occasion, for the same reason, to intercede with heaven, he would go to the same place in the forest and say: "Master of the Universe, listen! I do not know how to light the fire, but I am still able to say the prayer." And again, the miracle would be accomplished.

Still later, Rabbi Moshe-Leib of Sasov, in order to save his people once more, would go into the forest and say: "I do not know how to light the fire, I do not know the prayer, but I know the place and this must be sufficient."

Then it fell to Rabbi Israel of Rizhyn to overcome misfortune. Sitting in his armchair, his head in his hands, he spoke to God: "I am unable to light the fire and I do not know the prayer; I cannot even find the place in the forest. All I can do is to tell the story, and this must be sufficient." And it was sufficient.

God made man because He loves stories.[3]

The contemporary pilgrim is a person separated from the life-infusing myths that supported tribal man. He is a secular isolate celebrating the wake of a dead God. When God lived, and man belonged, psychology was no more than "a minor branch of the art of story-telling and mythmaking."[4] Today, each man must work at telling his own story if he is to be able to reclaim his personal identity.

Should he start out on a psychotherapeutic pilgrim-age, he sets out on an adventure in narration. Every-thing depends on the telling. The "principle of expla-nation consists of getting the story told—somehow, anyhow—in order to discover how it begins."[5] The basic presumption is that the telling of the tale will it-self yield good counsel. This second look at his personal history can transform a man from a creature trapped in his past to one who is freed by it. But the telling is not all.

Along the way, on his pilgrimage, each man must have the chance to tell his tale. And, as each man tells his tale, there must be another there to listen. But the other need not be a guru. He need only rise to the needs of the moment. There is an old saying that when-

ever two Jews meet, if one has a problem, the other
automatically becomes a rabbi.

But sometimes it is not enough for there simply to
be another to listen. A man not only needs someone to
hear his tale, but someone to care as well. This universal human need is touchingly revealed in the metaphor of the Legend of the *Lamed-Vov*.[6]

According to the ancient Jewish tradition of the
Lamed-Vov, there are at all times thirty-six hidden Just
Men, thirty-six secret saints upon whom the continued
existence of the world depends. When one dies another
takes his place. The Lamed-Vov are indistinguishable
from other human beings, except in the heartbreaking
depth of their caring. And only so long as the Just
Men exist, only so long as their special caring continues,
just so long will God allow the world of ordinary men
to continue to exist. So inconsolable are the Just Men
in their anguish about human suffering, that even God
Himself cannot comfort them. So it is, that as an act
of mercy toward them: "From time to time the Creator,
blessed be His Name, sets forward the clock of the Last
Judgment by one minute."[7]

The story is told about a young boy whose aging
grandfather informs him that the last Just Man has
died without designating a successor. The boy is to
take his place as one of the Lamed-Vov. He can soon
expect to attain the glow that is the aura of his coming
ascendency. The boy is awed, but bewildered as to what
he should do in this life as a Just Man. The old man
assures him that he need only be himself, that he need
not *do* anything to fulfill his destiny. In the meanwhile
he need only continue to be a good little boy.

But the child worries about his role, becoming obsessed with the idea that if he learns how to be a
Just Man, perhaps God will be satisfied and spare his
aging grandfather from dying. He fantasizes the grand
self-tortures and self-sacrifices that may be required of
him. Will he have to be dragged along the rough ground
clinging to the tail of a Mongol pony, or would it be

of greater merit if he were to be consumed by purifying flames while being burned at the stake?

He is terrified, but ready to do whatever is required of him. He decides to work his way up, beginning by holding his breath as long as he can. When this does not seem enough, he holds a match to his hand, burning his palm to a painfully satisfying stigmatic char. His grandfather is deeply upset and yet touched when he learns that the boy has been training himself to die in order to save the old man's life. He teaches the boy the nature of his monstrous error by explaining that as a Just Man, he will not be able to change anything. He will save no one. A Just Man need not pursue suffering. It will be there in the world for him as it is for each man. He need only be open to the suffering of others, knowing that he cannot change it. Without being able to save his brothers, he must let himself experience their pain, so that they need not suffer alone. This will change nothing for man, but it will make a difference to God.

The boy wanders off trying to understand, but not seeing the sense or the worth of it all. His epiphany comes later that day when he catches a fly whose life he holds in the hollow of his hand. He knows a sudden sympathy for the terror and the trembling of the fly. The fly's anguish is suddenly his own as well. Releasing the fly from his own trembling hand, he suddenly feels the glow of becoming one of the Lamed-Vov. He has become one of the Just Men. Love is more than simply being open to experiencing the anguish of another person's suffering. It is the willingness to live with the helpless knowing that we can do nothing to save the other from his pain.

As a psychotherapist, I am no longer willing to accept anyone as my patient to whose pain I do not feel vulnerable. If someone comes to me for help whom I do not experience as the sort of person who is likely to become personally important to me, I send him away. I am no Lamed-Vov. I do not live for God's

sake, but for my own. Every hour spent treating a
particular patient is an hour of my life as well. Much
of my life is over. Some of what is left is already filled
with the emptiness of my loneliness, that pain in each
of us that can from time to time be eased, but from
which there is no final escape, save death. And too, in
my life there are disappointments that I cannot evade,
frustrations that I do not choose, and losses that I am
helpless to do anything about. Some troubles, of course,
I bring on myself, but others fall out of the skies onto
my unprotected head, shattering my joys and darkening
my pleasures. It seems foolhardy not to try to take
what care of myself I can, and so I choose to work
only with patients about whom I feel hopeful in sharing
my time. There are some patients whom I believe I
could help, but whom I send away nonetheless, feeling
that being with them would not be good for me. If I
am not able to be open to their pain, I may perhaps
find professional satisfaction in working with them, but
no personal joy. It's a bad bargain, and one I am no
longer willing to make.

When I work with a patient, not only will I be hearing his tale, but I shall be telling him mine as well. If
we are to get anywhere, we must come to know one
another. One of the luxuries of being a psychotherapist
is that it helps to keep you honest. It's a bit like remaining in treatment all of your life. It helps me to remain
committed to telling and retelling my tale for the remainder of that pilgrimage that is my life. Research
in self-disclosure supports my own experience that the
personal openness of the guru facilitates and invites the
increased openness of the pilgrim.[8] But I operate not
to help the patient, but to help myself. It is from the
center of my own being that I am moved to share my
tale. That it turns out to be so helpful to the patient is
gravy. Whenever I make the mistake of giving a piece
of myself *in order* to get the patient to share more of
himself, he balks at the shoddy, self-righteous manipulative quality of my efforts. In recent years, most often
instead I trust my feelings, and do what I feel like doing

without trying to control its effect on the patient. When an untrusting patient speculates on whether I am being genuine or just using psychotherapeutic techniques, he finds me totally uninterested in the distinction. I have not wondered whether I am being genuine or technical for almost as long as I have given up wondering whether I am being selfish or unselfish. What's the difference? How can the answers to such questions possibly help me? I try to be guided by Carl Whitaker's advice to feed the patient not when he is crying that he is hungry, but only when I feel the milk overflowing from my own nipples.[9]

The mutual exchange of self-revelations between guru and pilgrim do, of course, give priority to those of the seeker. I am in some ways an expert paid to offer services. The patient, though he may not realize it, always knows better than I just where we should begin each session. Because of this, each session begins with my silent attention to his coming initiation of the hour's interaction. I have not begun a session myself since I was a patient. I operate as a counter-puncher, each movement being a response to the patient's words, gestures, or postures. Yet it is not simply a game, and I cannot move with confidence in the healing power of my metaphors without being firmly centered in my own inner feelings. I must begin by joining the patient in "the transparent way"[10] we are to walk together, by being transparent to myself.

In a non-selectively accepting way, I must allow my own changing being to be continuously disclosed to my consciousness. I must be ready to confront feelings and ideas within myself that are ugly, evil, and discrediting, if I am to receive the lovely, tender, decent aspects of myself. All of the good/bad, strong/weak, divine/ridiculous Janus faces must be seen, if I am to have any time to live with my mask off. And should I wear my mask too long, when I take it off and try to discard it, I may find that I have thrown my face away with it.

If I am transparent enough to myself, then I can

become less afraid of those hidden selves that my transparency may reveal to others. If I reveal myself without worrying about how others will respond, then some will care, though others may not. But who can love me, if no one knows me? I must risk it, or live alone. It is enough that I must die alone. I am determined to let down, whatever the risks, if it means that I may have whatever is there for me.

My own free decision to be transparent is a commitment to never-ending struggle. Before a man can be free, first he must choose freedom. *Then* the hard work begins. But if this commitment invites a like commitment in my patients, we can offer each other courage to go on, joining each other along the pilgrim's way, foregoing semblance for openness, and solitude for community.

As in all problems between myself and the other, I must begin by trying to straighten myself out. As with every other significant human interaction, "the most effective way to invite authentic disclosure from another is to take the risky lead and offer it oneself, first."[11] Though I believe that the only real danger lies in that which is hidden, disclosure of myself to myself must precede disclosure to the other. Often I reveal to the other without any certainty as to what I am getting into. I may be just as surprised (horrified or delighted) as the other at what emerges.

Yet in some basic way my awareness of what emerges from within me has the primary function of giving me the freedom/responsibility of choice as to which feelings I choose to move on (and which I do not) in any given instance. I am *not* committed to the encounter group ethos of random openness at every point. I reserve a right to privacy at any given moment, and I respect that right in others (including my patients). I do not wish to engage in the brutality that masquerades as indiscriminate frankness. The "philosophy of the here-and-now," of "you do your thing and I'll do mine," is not my thing unless I am willing to face the consequences of my acts, to eschew needless hurting of others, and to know that no matter how into myself I am, from time to time I will surely act like a fool.

Within those ambiguous parameters, I would come to know the other and come to be known to him. We will tell each other our tales, and we will be moved by the tales of others. As a child, I was so often lonely and out of it that if I had not found the tales of others in the books I read, I believe I would have died. Partly out of gratitude, I am regathering some of these tales that enabled me to survive. In these stories the pilgrim appears in varied contexts, wearing many guises. And as testimony to my own continued seeking, I have included an epilogue of the dreams that recount the story of my own continuing pilgrimage.

Part Two: Telling of the Tales

1. Tale of a Man Against the Gods

The oldest surviving work of fiction is the *Epic of Gilgamesh*.[1] There is no way of knowing how many generations of men told and retold the episodes of spiritual adventure in this long epic poem before it was finally written down. We can only be sure that about four thousand years ago, near the beginning of civilization in Mesopotamia, the tale of Gilgamesh was inscribed in cuneiform characters on twelve clay tablets, written in the ancient Semitic language, known as Akkadian. The tale was first deciphered at the British Museum less than a century ago. Though heralded as an archeological find, it is far more than that. It is a moving tale that lets me know that though he came and went thousands of years ago, yet this Sumerian king, Gilgamesh, is my brother.

Gilgamesh is strong, handsome, and wise, a great warrior, two-thirds god and one-third man. He rules his city, Uruk, whose great walls he has built, with power, with style, and with tyrannical cruelty. The men of Uruk are awed by his power and appalled by his arrogance. They complain:

> Gilgamesh leaves no son to his father;
> Day and night his outrageousness continues
> unrestrained.[2]

Though he is their shepherd, he oppresses them, till they can stand it no longer. So it is that they call upon the goddess Aruru, asking her to create a double for Gilgamesh, someone to equal his strength and the impetuosity of his heart. In this way, Gilgamesh may meet his match, be overcome, and leave the people of Uruk in peace.

In her wisdom, Aruru creates a double for Gilgamesh who will serve as his other half, his animal nature, someone who will break his pride by showing him that he is only a man. Each of us has such a shadow from which he flees. Each man is haunted by that specter of a double who represents all that he would say "no" to in himself. To whatever extent I deny my hidden twin-self, you may expect to see my personality twisted into a grotesque mask of neurotic caricature.

For the hyper-man like Gilgamesh who would stand above nature, the double is his animal self. Out of the clay Aruru fashions Enkidu, who knows nothing about people or land, who is dressed in the garb of the god of cattle and vegetation.

> His whole body is covered with hair . . .
> With the gazelles he eats grass;
> With the game he presses on to the drinking-place;
> With the animals his heart delights at the water.[3]

Each man has his Enkidu, his other half, his hidden self. The more he is out of touch with his double the more a man's life is an empty and unsatisfying burlesque. When such a man comes to me as a pilgrim/patient, then like the goddess, Aruru, I try to introduce him to his double, so that they may come to embrace one another. For one strong man who lives like a brute, there is the double of his own soft helplessness to be met. Without his weak and passive double, his capacity for tenderness and gentle touch is also lost. For another sort of half-man who meets the world as Mr. Nice Guy, there is the danger of living a life of self-degrading appeasement. In order to become free to assert himself when he needs to, he must first be introduced to the ruthlessly dangerous double of his undiscovered rage.

This is how mighty Gilgamesh comes to face his

double. While laying traps, a hunter comes upon Enkidu and flees in terror. The frightened hunter returns
to his village and breathlessly tells his father about this
hairy man-beast, who lives with the animals and tears
up man's traps. The hunter's father advises him to seek
the help of the mighty Gilgamesh in the city of Uruk.
Together they devise a devious plot to subdue the wild
man.

They select a beautiful prostitute, take her to the
water hole, point out Enkidu to her, and give her these
instructions:

> This is he, wench, naked at your bosom;
> Open your lap to him, so that he may succumb to your
>   beauty.
> Do not hesitate to approach him;
> When he sees you, he will approach you.
> Undo your robe and let him lie on you.
> Stir up lust in him, the woman's task.
> All living things, that are nurtured in their habitat, will
>   change their feelings towards him,
> When he shares his love with you.[4]

She does as she is instructed to do, and Enkidu is
roused as if possessed. They make love for six days
and seven nights. But then, when he is satisfied to leave
her and to return to the beasts, Enkidu finds that the
animals run from him, knowing now that he is not one
of them. He finds that he can no longer keep up with
them. He knows now that he is a man, no longer one
of the beasts.

It is fascinating to me to see that though the insight
into each person's double nature is central to the *Epic
of Gilgamesh,* there is as yet no understanding of the
dual sexual nature of each person. The myth of feminine evil is maintained. The female is the "dangerous
sex"[5] whose task it is to stir men's lust, but who in so
doing betrays them and robs them of their power.
When she is free she may operate independently against

men as a weapon, so it is necessary to bind her so that she may instead serve as a tool.

I would not argue that male and female personality characteristics are fundamentally the same. In the interests of the liberation of women (and reciprocally of men as well), we must attempt to sort out which characteristics (if any) are biologically intrinsic and which have been learned. It is only the acquired modes of gender that serve to maintain the oppression of sexual politics. Whatever the nature of these basic sexual differences, each person must come to own his double sexual nature.

In the *I Ching,* the primal power of maleness, symbolized by unbroken lines, is active, strong, spiritual, and light-giving. The female complement of male creativity is symbolized by broken lines. It is the dark, yielding, receptive power of the earth, the lusty completion of the superior male. For all the narrow, hostile misogyny implied in these contrasts, the *I Ching* offers some bits of wisdom in its juxtaposing of opposites. In the law of the Tao, the underlying concept is the idea of *change.* The apparent opposites, the yang and yin of male and female, light and dark, firm and yielding, all are forces arising out of change. There is never one pole without the other, no truth without a valid opposite, no going far enough in one direction without coming full circle.

No man can be fully a man unless he comes to terms with the female double within him. So too, with women and their male shadows. Those who do not know their sexual counterparts are absurd caricatures of the identities to which they aspire. Not knowing the hidden other within themselves, they hate and distrust the opposite sex. In this instance the Gilgamesh epic instructs by its badly flawed portrayal of women.

When Enkidu returns to the prostitute, she convinces him to come with her to Uruk. They set out to visit the holy temple, sacred home of the gods, and to meet and to challenge the mighty Gilgamesh.

When they arrive at the city, they find the young people in the streets, festively dressed, celebrating a holiday. In the marketplace they see Gilgamesh, preparing to enter the temple for the Festival of the First Night, in which as King of Uruk, he is to deflower the brides whom lesser men are marrying. Enkidu challenges Gilgamesh by blocking his path and not permitting him to enter. The struggle begins. The two warriors grapple and wrestle furiously, shattering the doorpost of the temple and shaking its walls. But as matching halves, they must recognize each other as equals. Each is humbled in the acknowledgment of the other, as they cease their struggle, embrace, and vow friendship to one another.

Gilgamesh proposes to his clay companion that they set out together to cut down a cedar tree in the sacred forest. This will be a dangerous expedition meant to destroy the evil guardian of the forest, the terrible Huwawa whose "roaring is like that of a flood-storm [and whose] . . . breath is death!" Armed with axes, bows, and swords, the two set out for the Land of Cedars, daring to face the giant Huwawa, the "terror to mortals."[6] On their way, each is able to admit to the other his weaknesses and fears, and so it is that they are able to comfort and to encourage each other. Enlightened by prophetic dreams, protected by the loving prayers of Gilgamesh's mother, and watched over by the gods, the companions are able to endure.

They travel ceaselessly until they reach the edge of the sacred forest. There they sleep, rising at dawn with axes in hand to cut down the cedar. The terrible Huwawa appears and is about to kill them. Gilgamesh calls out to the heavenly Shamash, the sun god. Once an arrogant tyrant, Gilgamesh has now become whole by joining with his animal half, his companion, Enkidu. Now he can be supported by the forces of nature in his holy quest. So it is that Shamash calls forth tempestuous winds to blind the monster by beating against his eyes, and to hold him so that he cannot go forward nor turn back. Huwawa pleads for mercy, but Gilgamesh and Enkidu do not listen. They kill the giant and cut off his head.

The heroes return to Uruk. Full of boasting, Gilgamesh washes and grooms himself, donning his magnificent royal robes and his jeweled golden crown. So fair is he that Ishtar, the goddess of womanhood, invites him to be her consort, promising him a life of splendor and luxury. But Gilgamesh refuses, berating Ishtar for her fickle ways, and for her cruelty to her previous lovers. She has loved a bird and then broken its wing; loved a horse then whipped him; loved a shepherd and then turned him into a wolf, now chased by his own herd-boys and bitten by his own dogs.

Furious at these insults, Ishtar flies to heaven to complain to her father, Anu. But Anu points out that she invities this treatment by behaving as cruelly as she does. Still she demands that he send the bull of heaven to destroy Gilgamesh. If he refuses, she threatens to smash the door of the underworld and release the dead who will outnumber the living. Anu cautions that if he gives in and sends down the bull of heaven there will be seven years of famine in the land. Ishtar convinces her father that she has stored enough food and fodder to save the people and their cattle. Anu gives in.

The bull of heaven, who could kill two hundred men with his first snort, descends to attack Gilgamesh and his warrior brother. Enkidu springs up, and seizing the bull of heaven by his horns, turns his charge, and then thrusts his sword into the nape of the bull's neck. Then the two tear out the bull's heart and present it to Shamash, the sun god.

Ishtar is enraged. "Woe unto Gilgamesh," she cries out, "who has besmirched me and has killed the bull of heaven."[7] Hearing her so credit only Gilgamesh, Enkidu, in prideful wrath, tears out the right thigh of the bull and tosses it at Ishtar, saying he would do the same to her if only he could.

Ishtar calls together all the prostitutes and courtesans to participate in the burial of the bull. But, at the same time, Gilgamesh calls together his artisans and his armorers, gathers up the remains of the bull and rides with them through the streets of Uruk to receive his people's tribute, saying:

> Gilgamesh is the most glorious among heros!
> Gilgamesh is the most eminent among men![8]

That night Enkidu has a prophetic dream that a council of the gods meets to judge and punish those prideful enough to slay both the bull of heaven and Huwawa, the guardian of the sacred forest. Before the council can decide who of the two is the more guilty, and so must die, Enkidu awakens, and tells Gilgamesh of his dream.

Gilgamesh insists that they are equally guilty of prideful exploits and of provocative boasting. Realizing that Enkidu is half of himself, Gilgamesh swears that he will spend the remainder of his life in mourning if Enkidu is put to death. Enkidu sickens, and as he lays dying, he reviews his life. He curses the hunter and the courtesan who tempted him to leave the wilderness, and blames them for bringing him to this awful pass. But Shamash appears and points out that these people also united him with Gilgamesh and brought him to glory. There is no gain without cost. Enkidu listens and understands. His angry heart grows quiet.

For twelve days Enkidu grows weaker, and at last he dies. Gilgamesh mourns as he would a dead younger brother, a part of himself, now lost forever. And, soon, as if for the first time, Gilgamesh realizes that someday he too will die. His power, his courage, and his wealth mean nothing. Nothing can save him from dying, and knowing this he grows frightened.

He decides to go to the mountain of Mashu to seek Utnapishtim, he who is reputed to hold the secret of immortality. He goes to this mountain:

Whose peaks reach as high as the "banks of heaven,"
And whose breast reaches down to the underworld.[9]

At the gate he is challenged by its guardian, the scorpion-man. Learning that Gilgamesh seeks the secret of eternal life from Utnapishtim, he warns him that no man has ever gotten through the long tunnel of darkness that leads there.

Nonetheless, Gilgamesh goes on and enters the tunnel. After many hours he emerges into a lush garden of jeweled trees. At a resting-house he meets Siduri, the barmaid, who questions him sympathetically about his quest. He tells of his pride and of the loss with which he has paid for it. She tries to help him to see the hopelessness of his venture, saying:

> The life which thou seekest thou wilt not find;
> For when the gods created mankind,
> They allotted death to mankind.
> . . . (Therefore) let thy belly be full;
> Day and night be thou merry;
> Make every day a day of rejoicing
> . . . This is the lot of mankind.[10]

But Gilgamesh is stubborn and will not be put off. He learns that to reach Utnapishtim, he must cross the Sea of Death to an island no man has ever reached. Urshanabi, the boatman of Utnapishtim, is also stopping at the resting-house and agrees to take him across the sea. But there is one stipulation. Gilgamesh's hands must not touch the waters of death. He must go to the forest and cut down one hundred and twenty punting-poles, for each one must be used just once and then discarded. They set out, and sail for a month, using up all of the poles. The last part of their voyage is completed with Gilgamesh's clothes raised as a sail on the mast.

At last, they arrive and Gilgamesh tells Utnapishtim his tale, and of his wish to live forever. But Utnapishtim points out that nothing lasts forever. He asks:

Do we build a house to stand forever? . . .
Does hatred remain in the land forever?
Does the river raise and carry the flood forever?
. . . From the days of old there is no permanence.[11]

In answer, Gilgamesh challenges his questioner who himself enjoys the immortality of a god. Utnapishtim reveals to him that in the distant past, at the behest of the gods, he had built an ark on which he had taken his wife and the seed of all living creatures. Then came a great flood, which did not subside for seven days. The ark came to rest on a mountain, and he discovered that all mankind had turned to clay. He sent out a swallow, but it could find no resting place, and so returned to the ark. Then he šent out a raven, and when it did not return, Utnapishtim knew that the waters had abated. In return for his faith the gods blessed them, saying:

Hitherto Utnapishtim has been but a man;
But now Utnapishtim and his wife shall be like us unto
    gods.[12]

Seeing that the gods would not do the same for him, Gilgamesh recognizes his disappointment and his weariness. He sleeps for seven days and seven nights. When he awakens, Utnapishtim feels sorry for him because he is so preoccupied with his dying. He tells him a secret of the gods, namely that there is a plant at the bottom of the sea that can give new life. Gilgamesh ties heavy stones to his feet, lowers himself into the sea, and finally finds the plant. But before he can eat it and become young again, the magic plant is snatched by a serpent. As the snake swallows the plant, its skin sloughs off to reveal a newer, younger skin beneath. This is how serpents learned to shed their old skins, thereby to renew their lives.

Gilgamesh sits down and weeps, realizing that all his efforts to overcome old age and death have gotten him nowhere. He takes this final disappointment as a

sign. It is useless to seek immortality. He must face the
fact of his own death, as all men must. He turns his
steps toward home, toward Uruk, where he must make
what he can of the rest of his life.

Like that of all other pilgrims, Gilgamesh's quest is
related to a search for the meaning of life. We all live
in a tragicomic situation, a life that is in part absurd
simply because it is not of our own making. We are
born into a disordered world, into a family we did not
choose, into circumstances we would have had somewhat improved, and we are even called by a name we
did not select.

Contemporary pilgrims, whose spiritual journeys
occur in the course of their psychotherapy experience,
have grown up in a Freudian age, which inspires them
to be much preoccupied with the conditions of their
childhoods for which they blame their current misery.
As with the rest of us, their childhoods were less than
perfect.

> Children are, after all, inevitably helpless and depen-
> dent, no matter what resources they may develop for
> coping with that towering world in which they live.
> Parents always turn out to be a disappointment, one
> way or another. Frustrations are many, and life is
> inherently unmanageable.[13]

Helpless as we all are as children, to change the
world, or to move on and take care of ourselves, we
must develop ways of pretending that we are not so
powerless. The fantasies developed in chidlhood, and
maintained right to the door of the therapist's office, are
termed "neuroses" in our Freudian age. But as we can
see in the *Epic of Gilgamesh,* men have always tried
to maintain illusions to protect themselves from living
with the anguish of their unimportant momentary existence and their helplessness to change the absurdity of
their needless suffering.

We are all May flies, or more poetically day flies,

those dainty insects with lacy wings and slender trailing tail, who live but for a day. The adult May fly lives only a few hours, just long enough to mate. He has neither mouth nor stomach, but needs neither since he does not live long enough to need to eat. The eggs the May fly leaves hatch after the parent has died. What is it all about. What's the point? There is no point. That's just the way it is. It is neither good nor bad. Life is mainly simply *inevitable*.

The patient/pilgrim insists that there must be some meaning that he just has not yet gotten hold of or else he would be happy. "Why?" he asks. "Why did all this happen to me?" He believes that if only he could understand, if only the therapist would explain it to him, then he could live with life as it is and be happy. But "the meaning of life can be revealed but never explained."[14] The point is that *there is no point*.

Perhaps the most difficult thing for the patient to accept is that he is quite *ordinary*. He and the therapist and everyone else he knows, all are just the same. In a world of three and one-half billion souls, countless numbers long dead and an infinite number yet to be born (if we don't succeed in blowing ourselves up or in poisoning our environment), how important are the momentary frustrations or satisfactions of any one of us?

The patient offers to make a deal. He will make me *special* if only I will let him be special. I am tempted, of course, but no deal! Every time I am lunatic enough to make that deal I regret it. Somehow, he always turns out to want to be more special than I get to be.

Of course, he does not believe that I can possibly believe that I am not special, that I am ordinary. This cannot be so, because I don't seem unhappy enough to believe that. "What do you *really* feel?" he insists. Perhaps I am lying to make him feel better. Perhaps it is really just a technique, a therapeutic ploy I am using to try to help him. I am only trying to help myself, to take care of myself, to maintain my sanity by not

letting him tempt me into the compact of our being
"special" (at least not more than briefly from time to
time).

I talk often of death, of his death and mine, and of
the deaths of the people we love. I will not let him
hide from the fact that we are both going to die, and
it will surely be too soon for either one of us. We will
be dead a long, long time. That will be it. There is
no meaning. It's a random universe, and time is short.
It slips by even as he wastes it complaining, feeling
sorry for himself, trying to be special, to be compen-
sated for his misfortunes.

At this point, I should make clear that all of this is
more vivid for me when I am on my own pilgrimage,
as a psychotherapist, than in the rest of my life. Each
session has a beginning, a middle, an end. We meet
only briefly each time, and at the end of the allotted
time, we stop. And someday we will separate; after
therapy we will never see each other again. That will
be it. Awareness of all of this keeps me in touch with
the ephemeral nature of each therapeutic encounter,
of the fleetingness of each coming together, and of the
brevity of my own life.

The central fact of my own life is my death. After
a while, it will all come to nothing. Whenever I have
the courage to face this, my priorities become clear.
At such times nothing is done *in order to* achieve something else. No energy is wasted on maintaining the
illusions. My image does not matter, I do not worry
about how I am doing. I do what I do, am who I am.
That's it. The imminence of my own death is the pivot
around which things turn. This makes what is going on
now all that counts.

Doing therapy is like remembering all the time that
you really are going to die. Because the therapy hour
has a definite beginning and ending, we are kept aware
of its being temporary. There is only *me,* and *you,*
and *here,* and *now.* We know in advance that it will
not last, and we agree to this. All relationships are temporary, but it is so terribly hard with my wife, my kids,

my friends, the people whom I love most, it's so terribly hard to remember that we have so little time. We stall, kid ourselves, promise that we will deal with things some time soon. Not only are there many things that we never get around to dealing with, but even when we do, there is so damn much waste in the process, so much unnecessary distance between ourselves and those with whom we try to make a life.

In therapy, it is often so different. Because I remember that the time is definitely and arbitrarily limited, I more consistently take those moments seriously. My awareness of each moment in the microcosm of the psychotherapeutic pilgrimage allows me to be more dependably a present, free, decent human being with my patients than I am in the rest of my life. Oh, I try to make it all of the time, but when I am not working, I am far more likely to fool myself, to indulge my cruelty, and to trip on my arrogance.

Too often, I forget that I am dying, that we each of us suffer from the same terminal disease. At such times, when I do not remember to remember, I blow it. The pilgrimage of Gilgamesh reminds me of "the absurdity of life and death, heroic wistfulness, nostalgia for lost possibilities, melancholy of missed perfection . . . [and that even] the love of comrades cannot prevail against the insult of death."[15] The pilgrimage of my brother, Gilgamesh, helps me not to forget.

2. Tale of a Spoiled Identity

Women are to blame for all the trouble in the world. The Bible tells us so.

When God confronted Adam in the Garden of Eden, He thundered the accusation: "Have you eaten of the tree, of which I commanded you not to eat?"[1] And Adam, trembling and ashamed in his nakedness, copped out: "The woman whom thou gavest to be with me, she gave me the fruit of the tree, and I ate."[2]

Because Adam had listened to the voice of his wife, instead of harking to the commands of the Lord, God was angry and condemned him to live from then on by the sweat of his brow. He would no longer take care of a man who had yielded to female domination. Eve was to suffer punishment as well, and additionally was to endure man's political domination forever. To the woman, God said: "I will greatly multiply your pain in childbearing; in pain you shall bring forth children, yet your desire shall be for your husband, and he shall rule over you."[3]

But there is an apocryphal interpretation of the myth of Creation, which suggests that Eve's formation from the rib of the lonely, sleeping Adam, was God's *second* attempt at finding him a helpmate. When God first "created man in his own image, in the image of God he created him,"[4] at the same time, "male and female he created them."[5]

An old Hebrew tradition holds that this first creation included a female called Lillith. She was the very first defender of the cause of women's liberation. When Adam told Lillith that she was to obey his wishes, she replied: "We are equal; we are made of the same earth."[6] So saying she flew up into the air and transformed herself into a demon who ate children. Even that early, women who would not subjugate themselves to the will of men were seen as witches.

To this day, women have remained the most consistent object of man's inhumane political and social oppression. Other groups rise and fall, but females remain oppressed, even when they no longer constitute a minority.

The female pilgrimage is an attempt by women to regain their status as full-fledged human beings, to be accepted as the natural equals of men, and no longer to be used as a repository for the projected evil that males thus disown. As a man, at times I am certainly a part of the conspiracy that has kept women degraded and unhappy. I no longer relish my part in this alleged supremacy. I am committed to the struggle toward freedom that the success of the female pilgrimage would provide for both men and women. But for all my good intentions, I am still more a part of the problem than of the solution. Though I support the Women's Liberation Movement, I will not attempt to speak for it. Women are no longer voiceless. They now speak out strongly for themselves.[7]

As a psychotherapist, I am particularly interested in that part of women's spoiled identity that is fostered by destructive family relationships. The roots of most of women's problems are political and social. The solution to such political problems must be revolutionary rather than psychotherapeutic. Psychoanalysts in particular have been justly accused of encouraging women to adjust to, rather than change, oppressive cultural conditions. They have suppressed the dissent of understandably unhappy women by classing them as "neurotics," in a way that makes no more sense than it would to impose such a diagnosis on ghetto-trapped blacks.

In my own work with female patients, I try to encourage them to sort out those parts of the problem that belong to all women, to seek the support of their sisterhood, to explore Women's Liberation Movement meetings if they wish, and to find political solutions for the political problems. Then, as I can, I work with them on the personal psychological aspects of their identity struggles.

My work with Willo has been a rewarding opportunity to join and to guide an unhappy young woman along the way of her pilgrimage toward freedom, self-respect, and appreciation of her personal worth. We have helped each other, and she has taught me to understand something of the nature of a woman's ordeal in the struggle to become whom she might be. I will let her speak for herself. She has learned to do that in ways that are both touching and powerful.

At Willo's request, I have not guarded her identity by giving her a fictitious name. She is proud of what she has become and generous in her willingness to share the moving experience of her own painful struggle with other spiritual pilgrims. Willo grew up feeling unsupported by her mother as she was thrust into the role of an enigmatic decoration for a father who was deeply committed to the pursuit of his own professional achievements. As an adult she was too often a self-discrediting support for her husband, helping him to do his thing, while settling for the meager reward of "security" for herself. Needless to say, she made him pay. For years she engaged in all of the self-degrading, secretly spiteful ways that women have developed to subtly victimize their oppressors. It is much like the passive resistance to white domination that Negroes so long practiced as "niggers," before they stood up to become blacks.

Early in therapy, for the most part Willo concentrated her struggle on new ways of defining her relationships with men. As part of her quest for an identity as a grown-up woman-person, she had to give up defining herself as some man's good girl or lovely wife. She had to wear a face of her own. There was much to be learned, and perhaps even more to be unlearned. But at least the enemy was clear, first as the cruelly insensitive Male, and then as her own stubborn need to be taken care of by Daddy.

She labored long and hard to emerge from the slime of an identity spoiled by the oppression of experiencing herself as a nonperson, born to be a helplessly trapped disappointment to a father who was not really interested in any child who could not immortalize his maleness. Though this is the family link most often emphasized in Women's Liberation Movement analyses of the degradation of the female ego, a young girl's sense of who she is in her mother's eyes is also a crucial parameter in the development of her stigmatized self. Willo's growing awareness of her resentment and longings in connection with being her father's daughter arose more readily than the more subtly stifled, insidiously vaguer self-dissatisfaction implied in having been her mother's girl.

The congested feelings deadened the joy in her. She could not scream them out. She did not own her rage. In order to facilitate a more vivid experience of these elusive feelings of hurt, of anger, and of longing, I suggested that she write a letter to her mother, a letter she need never mail. It was to be an attempt to make a claim on her mother, to speak out in that anguished voice that no one had ever heard.

For weeks, Willo stalled, panicked at the thought of experiencing her own dreaded feelings, which the writing of such a letter promised to unleash. She claimed that what was stopping her was the hopelessness that she would ever be heard. Should she write and send such a letter, the only response she could imagine receiving would be more of the same self-sorry, evasive denials and pap that had met all earlier attempts to reach out to her mother. Her inability to have any impact on her mother had been transformed into a sense of her own powerlessness, a paralyzing drain of futility.

I suggested that since this never-to-be-mailed letter was only a fantasy trip, rather than a political act, Willo was free to write mother's answering letter as well.

She might be able to release herself from the ambivalence on which she usually relied, if she could somehow separate her desperately tender longings from her depressing expectations. I recommended that she consider writing two separate replies from mother. The first would be the sort of response that had felt so devastating every time she had tried to get close to mother in the past. If she could get that out of the way, then perhaps she could write a second letter, the sort of reply that she had always wanted from her mother, but had never gotten. In any event, even fantasizing the possibilities of these two separate sorts of replies might free her to write her own unspoken cry to mother.

Finally, one day Willo began her individual therapy hour by handing me copies of these three letters, which she had finally managed to let herself write. I had not recommended this experiment as an attempt to garner more clinical information for myself, but rather as a way of providing an opportunity for Willo to get into more direct touch with her own feelings. And so, I turned the letters back to her without reading them. If she would be willing to read them aloud to me, she would come to know the feelings in still a new way, and I might share in her experience of reclaiming this lost part of her soul. She trusted me once more, and began to read the first letter, stopping only when, from time to time, she was crying so hard that she could not speak. The first letter began:

Dear Barbara:

I started to write "mother" out of habit . . . but Barbara seems more appropriate, as you never really have been a mother to me in the ways that I think are appropriate. A mother should nurture and protect her young, not eat them. A mother should touch and love her children physically and emotionally. We always had a thing in our house where we did not spank the kids. . . . I used to think that this was a great thing, that hitting a kid was a breach of trust . . .

however, I realize in our house it was just an extension of our not touching at all . . . not in anger or in love. Instead we were disciplined by a quiet sullen anger that would erupt in tirades that were isolating and destructive, and indicted the whole person. To this day if someone gets angry at me I equate it with their feeling me totally worthless and with their wanting to cut things off with me. I experience a panic on the edge of which I have lived all my life.

I used to think that you were the victim and such a weak, ineffectual woman whom life had dealt some cruel blows. You were really a goddamn slut who was manipulating everyone with your supposed helplessness. When I look back you sure were the victor who ended up with the spoils. Your possessions always meant more to you than anyone else . . . that's funny, I said "anyone" but to you they were animate . . . at least as animate as you were. You always lavished such care on the house, the car, your boat . . . and of course your poodle . . . but he offers no threat . . . time time time . . . time and money and things . . . that's your life. I could never understand why you were always running around saving time . . . it never seemed to me that you did anything with it . . . you don't read, you don't think . . . what is important to you . . . not your new husband, Bill . . . he is just another non-threatening object in your life that gives you the impression that you are not alone . . . but you are ALONE AND IT'S YOUR OWN GODDAMN FAULT. . . . It could have been different . . . when I was little I really needed you and if you could have been there for me instead of sacrificing me at the altar of my father . . . we could have a beautiful relationship now. A mature mother and daughter relationship instead of this.

When I think of you I get all squirmy and ughc . . . it's like you were completely decayed inside and if I really gave you a warm supportive loving hug . . . your walls that are a facade would crumble . . . you are a variation on Dorian Gray only yours is happening inside. . . . You are like a bacteria that cannot live in the presence of warmth and love . . . and real concern. I have paid too high a price to pretend that I have a mother . . . I don't . . . and I do not want to sacrifice my own daughter at your altar.

It was a while before she could go on beyond her gasping, anguished rage, before I was able to listen to more. The second letter was delivered as a mocking, openly cruel parody of all the empty replies her mother had ever offered. The reading began in a disturbingly nasal whine:

Dear Willo.

I was very disturbed by your recent letter. When you are a little older, Willo Ann, I think that you will understand more of the kinds of things that I did. It is not as easy as you younger people would like to think that it is. When your children are older you will find out what it is really like.

Bill and I went down to the boat for the weekend. . . . I baked a chocolate cake and 60 dozen cookies. I froze some of the cookies in little bags so that I can take out a dozen at a time when I need them. We have bought a new refrigerator for the boat and it is wonderful. We can take enough food down for the whole weekend. We took a cruise at night to look at the harbor lights.

Bill is going to take off the month of August so we can take a cruise. He has worked very hard this year and really needs the rest. We have been working in the yard every night when he gets home, trying to get it in shape. It was such a mess, you know, since we haven't gotten much rain.

I told you that we had the complete house repainted. It really needed it. It looked so awful. I have put up lovely ruffled curtains in the guest room . . . it was very expensive, and the painters worked so slowly. I could have done it faster myself and probably better but I just don't have the energy anymore. Anyway, it is really nice to have it done.

We haven't heard anything from your brother. I guess he is still up in Maine.

I have discovered a new recipe for Marshmallowed Marshmallows. It is really terrific. If I can find the recipe I'll send it to you. It's very quick to make and you can freeze it.

It's almost time to go back to school again. I am not looking forward to it. The kids just aren't the same. The town isn't like it used to be. They don't come from the nice families that they used to here. So many Mexicans and colored now, you know. If I can just get assigned to Home Ec., it's so easy because I have done it before, and hang on a few more years, I can retire.

Well, say hello to the kids for me.

> Love,
> Mother

Willo and I laughed and snickered in the new-found intimacy of a conspiracy of naughty children. Our snide vengeance spent, we turned toward the final fantasy letter, the reply Willo had always hoped for, and would never ever receive, the one she would have to do without. She read this one softly, with quiet tenderness:

Dear Willo.

I was very sad to receive your letter because it said so many things that I have known but have tried to hide from myself. I know that I was not a very good mother . . . I cannot even say that I tried very hard. I was so scared most of my life and was not really ready to be a mother or even a wife. I suppose I was only doing what I had seen my mother do and experience but someone has to stop the cycle. I am sorry that I could not be the one to do it. I am glad for you that you are trying to find something real for yourself . . . I am afraid that it may be too late for me. I am locked into a job and a marriage that are not satisfying for me but they do give me financial security. I grab onto things because I am terrified that I will be poor, old, ugly, stupid and alone.

You were such a cute little girl I regret that I did not enjoy you when you were small. Your own daughter reminds me so much of how you were. You should value this time with her because it will never come again. I know.

Young people seem to be fortunate today. They have so many choices that I didn't think were possible when I was young. Maybe that is just rationalizing why I didn't take more control of my own life in a real way. You are right that I sold out to the wrong things. In many ways I was more in control of my own life because I never let it happen; I always manipulated the situation. It only left me with a very empty, lonely life. It's ironic but in fact all the things that I feared have really come to pass.

I hope that it is not too late.

                                                    Love,
                                                    Mother

We cried softly. I thanked her for letting me come so close, for teaching me so much.

As Willo came to know and to value her own wishes during the course of psychotherapy, she began more and more to put her deadening security on the line. She reached out for her freedom. How delighted she was to be warmly received by a sisterhood of compassionate pilgrims. As her considerable creative imagination came to flower, one of the ways in which she asserted her rights was in the search for a career of her own. The piece that follows is part of her *Statement of Purpose,* an essay required by the graduate studies program to which she was applying:

I managed to get a bachelor of arts degree by pasting the right number of stamps on transcripts and turning them in at an accredited institution which awarded me the degree. It was a meaningless, directionless, end-gaining experience. In applying to be accepted as a graduate student, I am asking that you take a leap of faith with me. As a weaver, I am very improvisational, planning only the warp and allowing the design to take shape from the dynamic tension between the threads as I build up the weft. I trust that in the environment which this program would provide, my intellectual and emotional growth would create a dynamic tension and I, WILLO, would be in the real sense my own thesis.

I am going to begin my essay with that about myself which I feel will most hinder me because the essence of my statement of purpose is to overcome my feelings of inadequacy as a woman and in so doing, develop a system whereby I can help others accomplish this also.

The beginning of my handicap has its roots in the social structure but for my personal development it has its beginnings in my name, Willo. For years whenever anyone met me they would ask the orgin of my beautiful and unusual name. "I was to be my father's first son." I would reply glibly, "and when I arrived they had to change it from Willis, Jr." My parents might have feminized it to Willa but they neuterized it to Willo. It took me years to experience the irony and anguish in that anecdote which I tossed off so quickly. I have struggled so many years as the "neutered son" of an emotionally impotent father. I have raged against others because of the gnawing self-hatred that I have felt. I have diminished myself in most ways because of what my parents and society taught me was my worth as a woman and my perception of myself as a second-class man.

My audacity in applying for this innovative graduate program makes me realize that I have begun to lift myself out of the morass of feelings of inadequacy and worthlessness. However, I have come to recognize that the pain which I have and will continue to experience in coming to love myself will prove my greatest asset.

The graduate training at the Institute, with an emphasis on the symbiotic understandings "that individuals cannot be understood apart from the social contexts in which they live and that an understanding of social structures and processes depends in part on knowledge of personality dynamics," is crucial for me. I feel that I must understand the "essential core of psychology" and from this distill the myths that have enslaved and confined women in their own minds. My graduate study will be a personal odyssey of self-understanding and self-acceptance. I will then apply these perceptions in a therapy situation working with women and men as individuals and groups helping each to confront his or her own peculiar dilemma.

3. Tale of a Discontented Disciple

Siddhartha[1] is Hermann Hesse's lyrical novel, his poetic retelling of one of the legends of the spiritual journey of the Buddha. This Sanskrit word, *siddhartha,* means "he who has achieved his aim." It is the personal name of Gotama, the most recent of the Buddhas. But Hesse tells us that the tale of Siddhartha's pilgrimage is also his own: "All these stories dealt with me, reflected my own path, my own secret dreams and wishes, my own bitter anguish."[2]

This tale begins when Siddhartha, the beautiful son of a Brahman priest, finds that though he makes everyone else happy, he is not happy himself. He has spent much time in contemplation, in meditation, and in the silent pronunciation of Om. He has learned all that his father and the other wise Brahman teachers can offer him, but yet his insides are not full, "his intellect . . . not satisfied, his soul . . . not at peace, his heart . . . not still."[3] He is restless and discontented because his *knowledge* of Atman (the universal consciousness) does not satisfy him. He wishes to *experience* the Atman and comes to see that: "One must find the source within one's own Self."[4]

He and his father struggle with the anger and the sorrow of their separation, when Siddhartha decides to go into the forest with the wandering, ascetic seekers, the Samanas. These strange, self-denying men are "worn-out . . . , neither old nor young, with dusty and bleeding shoulders, practically naked, scorched by the sun, solitary, strange and hostile—lean jackals in the world of men."[5] His loving friend and "shadow," Govinda, joins Siddartha on his pilgrimage.

Frustrated with intellectual search, he gives himself over to three years of yoga and asceticism, abandoning the world of his senses as well, for a life of pain, exposure, and fasting. He wishes "to become empty . . . to let the Self die."[6] By killing his memory and his senses, he learns ways of losing his Self, only to find that to the Self he returns, again and again. Govinda suffers and begs at his side.

Siddhartha grows discouraged that these temporary escapes will ever allow him to achieve the tranquillity of Nirvana. He feels he has only learned tricks to deceive himself. He tells Govinda that a long time has been spent to learn a lesson that he has not yet finished learning: "that one can learn nothing."[7]

Hearing that an illustrious Buddha has appeared who wanders the countryside preaching to his disciples, Siddhartha decides to seek out this wise man. Govinda departs with him. Together they leave the forest and journey until they find the yellow-robed Buddha in the Grove of Jetavana. They listen to the holy man's teachings. Govinda is filled with wonder and decides to become a disciple. They separate because Siddhartha chooses "to leave all doctrines and all teachers and to reach . . . [his] goal alone—or die."[8] Searching for the Atman among the Samanas, he tried to escape from the Self, only to learn that it is the Self that he must discover and come to know. Now in the midst of seeking a teacher, he "has discovered that comforting secret that a teacher is unnecessary."[9]

The psychotherapy patient must also come to this heavy piece of understanding, that he does *not* need the therapist. The most important things that each man must learn, no one else can teach him. Once he accepts this disappointment, he will be able to stop depending on the therapist, the guru who turns out to be just another struggling human being. Illusions die hard, and it is painful to yield to the insight that a grown-up can be no man's disciple. This discovery does not mark the end of the search, but a new beginning.

So it is that Siddhartha leaves the grove (and his

youth) behind, feeling himself to be a man. Now he knows that he can only learn the secret of Siddhartha by becoming his own teacher. He is as one awakened, filling his senses with the beauty of a world he had so recently termed an "illusion." He would have a new life. It is his to choose.

Siddhartha looks and listens, he tastes and smells and touches. Now he is present and belongs to the world. He hungers for new experiences. And so he travels on to the large and busy city of Sansara. There he seeks out the beautiful courtesan, Kamala, and asks that she instruct him in the art of love. She will not, for he lacks clothes, shoes, and money. He cannot yet command the pleasures he wants from her. When he suggests that he could hurt her and rob her of them, she points out that he could no more do this than she could take the wisdom of a Samana from him against his will. Each must be given willingly or "not one drop of sweetness will you obtain from them."[10]

How is he to earn the money she requires? His only talents are to think, to wait, and to fast; none of them are salable. Then he remembers one other talent: he can compose poetry. He offers this verse to her:

Into her grove went the fair Kamala,
At the entrance to grove stood the brown Samana.
As he saw the lotus flower,
Deeply he bowed.
Smiling, acknowledged Kamala,
Better, thought the young Samana
To make sacrifices to the fair Kamala
Than to offer sacrifices to the gods.[11]

Kamala is delighted, and in return, she teaches him the varied pleasures of love. They are happy together, as she shows him that "one cannot have pleasure without giving it."[12]

Kamala introduces Siddhartha to the wealthy merchant, Kamaswami. Together they instruct the young pilgrim in the ways of the world, of money and the flesh. He stays on, enjoying his growing store of riches and a variety of sensual pleasures. Lulled by a life of luxury, Siddhartha searches no more. Then one morning, sleeping late abed, he dreams about:

> . . . a small, rare songbird [which Kamala kept] in a small, golden cage. . . . This bird, which usually sang in the morning, became mute, and as this surprised him, he went up to the cage and looked inside. The little bird was dead and lay stiff on the floor. He took it out, held it a moment in his hand and then threw it away on the road, and at the same moment he was horrified and his heart ached as if he had thrown away with this dead bird all that was good and of value in himself.[18]

Psychotherapy patients also soon learn to be moved by their nocturnal visions as they discover that we are often wiser when we dream than when we are awake. Because the dreaming experience is unhampered by whorish Reason, and the dreamer is not distracted by the conventional wisdom of other people's perspectives and expectations, we sometimes see most clearly when our eyes are closed.

I encourage my patients to dream more, to remember what they have dreamt, and to share their experiences with me. This I do by revealing to them accounts of my own dreams, particularly the dreams I have about them. If the patient accepts my invitation to participate in such a dialogue of midnight reveries, we sometimes engage in a series of echoing dreams. We alternately call out to and respond to one another, by finding that each in turn dreams a dream that relates to the other's last shared experience.

In these exchanges, patients fear most the out-of-control, upsetting "bad dreams." It is difficult for them to accept that *nightmares are simply those dreams that we are too frightened to complete*. We panic. The fear that we will confront something that will face us with more terror than we can bear leads us to escape into waking, still haunted by the awful bad-dream feelings. It is like a person having a "bad trip" when he drops acid (LSD). Going on a "bummer" is "not so much a matter of actually running into something terrible within oneself, as it is a terror-stricken flight from whatever it is that one might encounter in the unplumbed depths of one's mind."[14] I encourage patients to complete their nightmares in fantasy trips during the therapy session. Some come to be able to redream them more fully at night and in so doing find relief and fulfillment in their once-dreaded nightmares.

Through his dream, Siddhartha becomes aware that the path of luxury and sensual pleasure is as foolish as that of asceticism. Greed and gambling have possessed him without fulfilling him. And as for Kamala: "Sexual love is an art, and art is a game; every game is dangerous, for the player may sooner or later forget it is a game."[15]

Siddhartha steals away from the city of Sansara without saying he is leaving. When Kamala learns that he has left, she weeps to realize that he remains a homeless pilgrim. She goes to her golden cage, opens the door, releases her rare songbird, and lets it fly away. Siddhartha has left without knowing that Kamala carries his child.

After leaving the city, he wanders aimlessly through the forest. Tired and hungry, he finds himself at the river. Filled with despair, empty of purpose, he thinks to commit suicide by drowning himself. He is stopped by some stirring of his old self, as "from a remote part of his soul, from the past of his tired life, he heard a sound . . . the holy Om."[16] Realizing the folly of seeking peace by destroying his body, he reaches for the inward perfection of the silently pronounced "Om," and falls into the refreshing, dreamless sleep of enlightenment.

He wakes to see a yellow-robed monk with shaven head, who turns out to be his old friend, Govinda. He finds it hard to believe that anyone dressed so elegantly as Siddhartha can possibly be on a pilgrimage. Sid-

dhartha tries to explain that he has lost his riches, but
Govinda is dubious, and goes on alone. The well-
dressed pilgrim reflects on his situation and realizes
that he has lost his worldly self just as, long before,
he had lost his ascetic self. Now he has nothing! He
knows nothing! He has learned nothing! Now, though
no longer young, he must begin like a child again. But,
rather than feeling grief, he:

> . . . felt a great desire to laugh, to laugh at himself, to
> laugh at this strange, foolish world.
>   Things are going backwards with you, he said to
> himself, and laughed, and as he said it, his glance
> lighted on the river, and he saw the river also flowing
> continually backwards, singing merrily.[17]

He is like a joyful child-person once more. Laughter
is the sound of freedom. Siddhartha "no longer merely
knows about, he *understands* the evils of the worldly
life" and so he is free of them.[18] His petty, prideful
self has died, and he is well rid of it. Siddhartha the
Brahman has died. Siddhartha the Samana has died.
Siddhartha the profligate sensualist has died. Siddhartha
lives!

He decides to live by the lovely river and to learn
from it. The wise ferryman, Vasudeva, befriends him
and helps him to learn the many secrets of the river.
He has already learned the value of seeking the depths.
He also comes to realize that the river is everywhere
at the same time, in the mountains, through the land,
and in the sea. It teaches that "there is no such thing
as time."[19] So too, Siddhartha the boy, Siddhartha the
youth, and Siddhartha the man are only separated by
shadows, not by reality. So too, is it with Life and
Death. "Nothing was, nothing will be, everything has
reality and presence."[20]

This understanding frees Siddhartha from sorrow.
He learns to open himself to listening to the river and
hears its many voices. He hears the voice of every living creature and its voice, and when he can hear all

of its ten thousand voices at the same time, it comes to him as the sound of Om. In this, he "learns of the totality and simultaneity of all being—man and nature alike."[21]

Siddhartha and Vasudeva live as holy men beside the river. Other pilgrims come and tell their tales, and are illumined by learning to be quiet so that they may listen to the river.

After twelve years, many pilgrims come to make a pilgrimage to the Buddha, who is dying. One among them is Kamala, the now-aging courtesan. She has brought Siddhartha's son along with her. Kamala dies beside the river from the bite of a snake, and Siddhartha begins to take care of the boy.

The boy turns out to be Siddhartha's final trial. He is a spoiled child of the city who only wants to get away from the quiet life by the river. The grieving boy becomes desperately important to Siddhartha, even as *he* had been to his own father. He does not want to give him up to Sansara. The river laughs, knowing that everyone must go to Sansara. As the boy revolts against Siddhartha's authority, "the father perceives the inevitability of the son's departure, of his son's corruption by the world."[22] The boy leaves. Siddhartha aches with longing.

After a time, Siddhartha learns to live with things as they are, beside the river, ferrying other pilgrims. He learns that wisdom is "nothing but a preparation of the soul, a capacity, a secret art of thinking, feeling, and breathing thoughts of unity at every moment of life."[23] He and Vasudeva continue to listen to the river. Siddhartha hears the voices of his youth, of all the people he had cared about and lost. He hears the voices flow to the sea, sees the river water become vapor, rise up to the sky and fall again as rain and dew. He sees that no thing and no one is lost. He hears the Om of the perfect unity of all things. Vasudeva goes off to the woods to die, and Siddhartha does not mourn him.

Govinda, his old friend, stops by. He questions Siddhartha about his enlightenment and is puzzled to dis-

cover that he claims to have learned what he knows
from a beautiful courtesan, a rich merchant, a dice-
player, and a boatman, and from listening to the river.
Govinda asks him for some knowledge, but Siddhartha
tells him: "Wisdom is not communicable. The wisdom
which a wise man tries to communicate always sounds
foolish."[24] There is nothing to tell because the distinc-
tions between things are illusions. "Truth cannot be
taught . . . [because] the paradox of paradoxes [is] that
of each truth the opposite is equally true.[25]

Govinda bends to kiss his friend, and in Siddhartha's
face, he sees a continuous stream of other faces, faces
of other people, of animals, of things. He sees that
Siddhartha has achieved the Buddha-hood, for his smile
reminds Govinda of "everything that he has ever loved
in his life, of everything that had ever been of value
and holy in his life."[26]

Before Siddhartha could discover that he needed no
teacher, he first had to exhaust his longing for others to
guide him, to take charge of his life. So too, with the
patient in psychotherapy and with every one of us. Unwilling to tolerate life's ambiguity, its unresolvability, its
inevitability, we search for certainty, demanding that
someone else must provide it. Stubbornly, relentlessly,
we seek the wise man, the wizard, the good parent,
someone else who will show us the way.

Surely *someone* must know. It simply cannot be that
life is just what it appears to be, that there are no hidden meanings, that this is it, just this and nothing more.
It's not fair, not enough! We cannot possibly bear having to live life as it is, without reassurance, without
being special, without even being offered some comforting explanations. Come on now! Come across!
You've got to give us something to make it all right.
The medicine tastes lousy. Why should we have to
swallow it just because it's the only thing we *can* do?
Can't you at least promise us that we will have to
take it just once, that it won't taste *that* bad, that we
will feel just fine immediately afterward, that we will

be glad we took it? No? Well then, surely, at least you have to give us a lollipop for being good.

But what if we are talking to ourselves? What if there is no one out there listening? What if for each of us the only wise man, the only wizard, the only good parent we will ever have is our own helpless, vulnerable self? What then?

This struggle of Siddhartha's is like the first phase of treatment for that other spiritual pilgrim, the psychotherapy patient. He will not have it any other way but that I (as his therapist) am bigger, stronger, wiser than he is. I must rescue him, instruct him, teach him how to live. But Lord help me if I try. He will show me that in the long run my efforts are not sufficient, that he is not satisfied. His resentment will surface as vengeance against the original parent who did not give him everything he wanted, who did not take care of him, completely and forever. I will now be punished for trying to be that good parent, coming with too little and too late. Where was I when he needed me most? Now he will make me feel as helpless and insufficient as he himself has felt.

I, of course, have tried to cure my own loneliness and helplessness by becoming a psychotherapist. If I cannot *have* the good parent, at least I can *become* the good parent. When I am hungry, I can feed the child in myself by instructing my patient-disciple. If he and I can get past this lunacy (we do not always make it), only then can he become curious enough about the possibilities of instructing himself to become his own disciple, to have what he might of his life as it is. That will also be my opportunity to give up trying to teach him. Instead, I can join him on his pilgrimage, more as another, more experienced pilgrim than as a guide. Then, like two lost children, we may comfort each other enough to maintain the courage to continue the search for home. For each of us, the only hope resides in his own efforts, in completing his own story, not in the other's interpretation. I must retrace my own

steps to find my way home. No one else's way can get
me there.

When Siddhartha, the patient, myself as therapist
(and you, too) realize that a teacher is irrelevant to
learning, then each of us must turn to himself. But we
must remember that we cannot move in one direction
without temporarily taking on the loss of another. People "cannot turn their backs to the shade without having the sun on their bellies."[27]

And in this turning, we each must go as far as we
can in reclaiming any part of ourselves that we have till
then disowned. So it is in Siddhartha's searching out
the limits first of his ascetic self, and then of his
sensual self. It is not possible to know how much is
just enough, until we have experienced how much is
more than enough.

The psychotherapy patient is also encouraged to give
in to himself, if he is ever to be free of himself. You
cannot get out of a trap unless you first get into it.
Overcoming by yielding is the only escape. So it is
that when a patient says he feels stuck and confused,
and through good intentions he struggles to become
loose and clear, he only remains chronically trapped in
the mire of his own stubbornness. If instead he will go
with where he is, only then is there hope. If he will let
himself get deeply into the experience of being stuck,
only then will he reclaim that part of himself that is
holding him. Only if he will give up trying to control
his thinking, and let himself sink into his confusion,
only then will things become clear.

Lao Tzu tells us that:

> What is in the end to be shrunk
> Must first be stretched.
> Whatever is to be weakened
> Must begin by being made strong.
> What is to be overthrown
> Must begin by being set up.
> He who would be a taker

Must begin as a giver.
This is called "dimming" one's light.[28]

Finally, Siddhartha learns to be still and to listen to the river of life. Patients learn in the course of telling their tales that they can discover themselves by becoming curious about the other struggling human beings with whom they live in the world. The only times that we can have what we long for are those moments when we stop grasping for it. At such times, all things are possible: *"to a mind that is 'still' the whole universe surrenders."*[29]

4. Tale of a Quest for Love

During the Middle Ages, everyone knew that it had been in the spring that the earth was first created. And so spring was a good time of the year to begin things, and a most fitting time to start out on a venture as holy as a pilgrimage to Canterbury.

Then too, with winter ending, it was a relief to be done with dark castles, too little heat, and a dull diet of light foods. It's little wonder that:

> When in April the sweet showers fall
> . . . .
> Then people long to go on pilgrimages
> And palmers long to seek the stranger strands
> Of far-off saints, hallowed in sundry lands.
> And specially, from every shire's end
> In England, down to Canterbury they wend.[1]

Chaucer's fourteenth-century *Canterbury Tales* form the last of the medieval pilgrim literature, with the pilgrimage itself serving as a framework story, which binds together the individual tales. Twenty-nine other pilgrims, and Chaucer himself, start out at an easy pace, riding fifteen miles each day of their three-day journey. To amuse and enlighten one another, each is to tell one story on the way, and another on the return.

Among the pilgrims are many types of people, representatives of almost every social class. They include, among others, a knight, a miller, and a cook, a man of law, a shipman, a nun and a monk, as well as a physician and a friar, a yeoman and a clerk. Each is described and comes alive through the earthy perspective

66

of Chaucer's own tough-minded yet highly civilized realism. Our host is a man who accepts all that is human, "enjoys everything and respects nothing."[2] He apologizes to the gentry and to the church, lest he has offended, but only as a further bit of political irony.

The characters themselves often take out their dislikes by derogatory stories about the jobs and positions of one another. It is out of the clashes of the personalities on the trip that some of the stories grow. And so it is that this literal pilgrimage mirrors the pilgrimage of human life. Geoffrey Chaucer's "wise, sure-eyed, and sensitive selection of daily detail, mellowed and harmonized by a humane and often amused approval, qualified . . . by an ironical wit"[3] make his pilgrims live even now.

The most memorable of them is The Wife of Bath. This lusty woman, Dame Alice, has spent her life engaged in the dance of love, with five husbands, "apart from other company in her youth," those "cocky lads." On her way to Canterbury, she is even then dressed for her primary pilgrimage in scarlet stockings "gartered tight," a big floppy hat "broad as . . . a shield," a flowing cloak over her large hips, and "ten pound" of colorful kerchieves.[4]

She is glad to have the opportunity to tell of the misery and woes of marriage and of the delicious joys of love-making. Experience is authority enough for Dame Alice. She has little use for celibacy. Religious mores of the time are misleading.

> Had God commanded maidenhood to all
> Marriage would be condemned beyond recall,
> And certainly if seed were never sown
> How ever could virginity be grown?[5]

Besides, virginity was intended only for those who wished to lead the perfect life. It is advised, not commanded. As for herself, Dame Alice is unwilling to forgo the honey and the flower of life for some senseless ideal.

She has always been a willing wife, since the age of twelve, always happy to offer her *"belle chose . . . whenever he wanted it."*[6] Her first three husbands (to each of whom she was unfaithful) were old when she was young, rich at a time when she was poor. She received their money and their lands, had her fun, did little to court their favor, and treated them to shrewish nagging. She would only be sweet to them once they had submitted to her domination.

Burying each in turn, she married a fourth, a playboy whom she thinks she loved best because he was "disdainful in love."[7] And when he died, at his funeral, she was attracted to a young Oxford clerk. Marrying for this fifth time, it was now *her* turn to be the older, the wealthier, and the more abused of the two. She was forty and he only twenty, but he was most unamorous, preferring to spend his time reading anti-feminist literature. Finally they had a fistfight over his neglect and contempt. She pretended he had killed her, "coming to" only once he showed remorse. Because he gave in, from then on she was kind to him.

Such exquisitely tortuous struggles between the sexes continue to be played out most elaborately in the lovely/awful, long-term compact called "marriage." Nonetheless, lifetime commitment to monogamous union seems to me the most rewarding alternative available in our present culture. I certainly wish to be open to the other alternatives, which are being suggested by the articulate spokesmen and spokeswomen of the sexual revolution, women's liberation, and communal living, but I do confess to finding it hard to believe that new solutions will not engender new problems. At present, I see monogamous, lifelong marriage as our most viable solution to loneliness, as the best setting so far available in which to raise children, and as the most practical contract for mutual support and freedom in a world so difficult for any one person to manage within.

Of course, marriage is also limiting, frustrating, and periodically terribly painful. Part of this, I believe, simply reflects how incredibly difficult it is to share the center of one's life with another completely separate, self-of-his-own human being. I am not even sure that the rewards ever clearly outweigh the difficulties. But with marriage, as with working for a living, there is little point in tallying up the credits and the debits to find out whether or not you are satisfied, unless there is another live possibility for solution. Certainly, you can (and in some cases it is wise to) find a new job or a new mate. But at the moment, long-term commitments to being out of work, or to remaining single, seem to create greater problems than they solve.

Many of the people who seek my help as a psychotherapist are troubled by the pain of marital difficulties. Ironically, in these willful struggles, a spouse often complains bitterly about having to live with a mate who is acting in just the ways that he (or she) found most attractive during courtship.

The wife, for example, once delighted to have found such a mate, now feels disappointed and lonely. When she first met her husband, she was attracted by his stability, his capacity for self-control, and his sensibleness. It was clear and pleasing to her that he could not be easily upset, that he was "objective" in outlook, and that he was very, very practical. His considered detachment made it seem that he could be counted on to protect her from her own harebrained impulsivity, and to see to it that she did not make an awful mess of things. What a terrible disappointment he turned out to be! Now she finds that he is cold, ungiving, and stodgy; he stubbornly ignores her feelings, and is no fun to be with.

This pejorative description of shortcomings that were once seen as virtues is not at all restricted to the female side of the struggle. Her husband once considered himself both wise and fortunate to have discovered a woman who was so alive and free emotionally, so enthusiastic, affectionate, and overflowing with energy. Now he is fed up. She has turned out to be impractical and impossibly demanding, asking more than anyone could give, never satisfied, and carrying on irrationally when she doesn't get what she wants.

He, of course, meets this onslaught first by trying to be "reasonable," and then by withdrawing into prolonged, thoughtful silences. He cannot understand why his detachment does not calm her down, any more than she can understand why he does not respond to her loneliness when she expresses it by crying pitifully, or by screaming, "All you ever do is watch the damn ball games on T.V." Each wants to get his (her) own way without being vulnerable, lest he (she) be seen as "giving in."

What people look for in marriage, at least in part, is the other half of themselves. Each of us is in some measure incomplete, with some aspects of our humanity over-developed and others neglected. What we do not claim for ourselves, we look for in the other (for example, aggressiveness, tenderness, spontaneity, stability, and so on). This is most extreme in the marriages of neurotics whose own self-image is so skewed that they seek out mates who are caricatures of the other end of the personality spectrum (such as the timid, self-inhibiting woman who searches for a glamorous, super-adventuresome epic-hero of a man, while he in turn seeks a woman too scared to let him get into trouble).

To some extent, each of us marries to make up for his own deficiencies. As a child, no one can stand alone against his family and the community, and in all but the most extreme instances, he is in no position to leave and to set up a life elsewhere. In order to survive as children, we have all had to exaggerate those aspects of ourselves that pleased those on whom we depended, and to disown those attitudes and behaviors that were unacceptable to them. As a result, to varying degrees, we have each grown into disproportionate configurations of what we could be as human beings. What we lack, we seek out and then struggle against in those whom we select as mates. We marry the other because he (or she) is different from us, and then we complain, "Why can't he (she) be more like me?"

If we married spouses who were like ourselves to begin with, other sorts of disasters might well ensue. For example, two timid souls would bolster each other's cautiousness till neither ventured to try anything new, while an adventuresome pair might escalate each other's recklessness into a spiral of catastrophes. Like it or not, these same differences between spouses are both the strengths of a good marriage and the hazards of a bad one.

In working with a struggling couple, I may point this out by asking the adventuresome husband: "Just what would happen if your wife said, 'Fine, go ahead!' every time you spun out one of your impulsive flights of fancy?"; or to the cautious wife: "Where would you get if your husband met your doubts with doubts of his own, so that you could stay stuck, instead of being encouraged to proceed, no matter how reluctantly?"

One way of conceiving the origins of these struggles is in terms of how children shape their identities in their relationships with their parents. What I am about to say about a boy's identification with his parents applies to the emergence of a girl's personality as well. And, too, obviously the identifications need not be with the parent of the same sex. Granting these variations, consider the oversimplified example of a boy identifying with a detached, passive, overly controlled father. His mother is likely to be aggressive and dramatically emotional. When the boy grows up, he will marry someone who is like the parent with whom he did *not* identify (aggressive mother). Soon the very qualities that attracted him will seem oppressive, and he will insist that she become more like the parent with whom he did identify (the passive, detached father). Ironically, should she try to comply; he will complain about the changes as being too little, or too late, or somehow not quite what he had in mind.

I used to wonder why there is so much marital difficulty. Now that I am more aware of the willful ways in which we are all tempted to struggle spitefully to get our own way, it amazes me that we are so often successful in our quest for love.

The Wife of Bath's autobiographical account of multiple marriages is merely a prologue to her chosen pilgrimage tale. The story she tells to the other pilgrims is another recounting of a struggle for sexual mastery in the quest for love, this time proceeding from rape, to marriage, to everlasting devotion. In this tale, "the world-wide scene of the quest dwindles to the marriage-bed of the dilemma."[8]

The tale begins in the good old days when King Arthur rules, before the elves and fairies of the land gave way to the purging holy friars. One of Arthur's young knights came upon a lovely young girl in the woods and "by very force he took her maidenhead."[9] For this rape, he was condemned to have his own head forcibly removed. The Queen and her ladies-in-waiting pleaded for his life, and so Arthur agreed to let the Queen decide the young knight's fate.

The Queen set up a condition under which he might be pardoned. She set him a task to be fulfilled in a year and a day, saying:

> Yet you shall live if you can answer me:
> *What is the thing that women most desire!*[10]

If not, then he must die!

For almost a year he searched the land, knocking at every door, asking his question, and receiving many, many answers, none of which he could count as right. What it was that women want most, he was told, is "wealth and treasure . . . honour . . . , jollity and pleasure . . . , gorgeous clothes . . . , fun in bed . . . , to be oft widowed and remarried . . . , [to be] flattered . . . ," and "freedom to do exactly as we please."[11] Near the end of the year, he felt no nearer to the secret truth than he had been at the beginning.

Finally, his time almost up, he rode home in dejection. As he came to the edge of a wood, he spied twenty-four ladies dancing on a green. He hoped that this might offer one last chance for him to learn the answer to the Queen's question, but as he approached, the lovely dancers vanished. In their place, there remained only an ugly old hag. She asked what he was looking for, and he told her of his quest. She promised him the answer to his question if, when he received it, he would swear to do whatever she should next require of him. Overcoming his revulsion, he took the old crone's hand, and agreed, upon his honor. And so it was that she revealed the secret to him.

The old woman and the knight rode to the Court together. The Queen asked the knight whether his search had been successful, and if so, commanded that he speak the answer. He spoke out, saying:

> A woman wants the self-same *sovereignty*
> Over her husband as over her lover.[12]

All the ladies were delighted with his answer, and agreed that his life would be spared.

The old woman sprang up and told the assemblage of her compact with the knight. She then turned to him, saying: ". . . keep your word and take me for your wife."[13] The young man was horrified and begged to be let off, to be subjected to some other demand instead. "Take all my goods, but leave my body free," he pleaded. But, alas, "he was forced to wed."[14]

On the joyless bridal bed, the young knight writhed in anguish, in "torture that his wife looked so foul."[15] The old woman felt hurt when he told her that he could not stand her because she was so old, and so ugly, and so low-bred. She insisted that all these matters of appearance counted for nothing. In fact, she went on to point out that, given all this, he would not have to worry about her being unfaithful.

Nonetheless, she would compromise, if need be. She offered him two choices: *either* he could have her old and ugly and faithful till she died, *or* she could change herself into a young and pretty and faithless wife. He needed only to choose.

He could not choose between two such grim alternatives. Instead he gave himself over to her sovereignty, leaving it to her to make the choice. At the moment when she knew that she had won mastery, she demanded that he kiss her. And just as he submitted, she turned all at once into a lovely young woman. Not only that, but she relented and swore to be faithful forever. And to his kisses,

> ... she responded in the fullest measure
> With all that could delight or give him pleasure.[16]

Like Dame Alice, many of the latter-day seekers, now on psychotherapeutic pilgrimages, are also much preoccupied with the struggle between the sexes. Psychoanalytic theorists tend to understand the plethora of sexual problems among patients as an expression of the unresolved infantile meanderings of the libido (that hypothetical fundamental sexual energy, the alleged instinctual basis of all behavior). I have no idea what proportion of the problems of sexual *struggle* may be instinctual. It is, however, clear that there are other influences afoot. The long-needed contemporary Women's Liberation literature, for instance, points up the oppressive politics of sex, the brutal oppression of women, the reciprocal entrapment of men in their own power-perversity, and the destructive counter-ploys that women have had to develop.[17] It may be that, if a man or a woman grows up in a culture as oppressive as ours, he (she) can no more be completely straight about sex than any of us can be about relationship between the races. Even as I dare to write about such issues, as a man, I must keep in mind that there are many ways in which I can never hope to really understand what it is like to be a woman in our culture.

Another set of parameters crucial to the sexual struggle is the expression of personal rather than social interactions. That so much human struggle seems to take place in sexual terms is somewhat misleading (by "sexual" here I mean a whole range of relatings between men and woman, not simply the explicit pleasures of the bedroom). The ambiguity and uncertainties of fulfilling oneself as a man or as a woman sometimes mask the more profound anguish of simply being human.

The ubiquity of such struggles occurs, *not* because of some fundamentally *problematic quality* of sexuality, but on the contrary, because sexuality has qualities that draw other problems to it as *people seek sexual solutions* for the never-ending conflicts and ambiguities of the hassle of living life as a human being, whether male or female. The entangled relationship between the sexes is the site of attempted solutions, which give the appearance of "problems" only because the solutions are unsuitable. *Sex is an arena* within which other kinds of problems get played out.

The first factor underlying the ubiquity of sexual conflicts within and between a man and woman is that sexual longings are to some extent instinctual, and therefore *dependable*. That is, they can reliably be expected to occur in everyone.

Second, sexuality is an *expendable* instinctual need. Hunger and thirst, for instance, though dependably present in everyone, cannot be messed with. These instinctual needs cannot long be denied without our destroying ourselves. They lack the logistical malleability of sex. Imagine trying to "hold out" on a partner by giving up food and drink for weeks!

A third fortuitous quality, which makes sex a likely instinctual arena for the acting out of other (non-sexual) conflicts, is that of all the instincts, sexuality seems to be the only one that is somehow fundamentally *interpersonal*. Even masturbation usually has an interpersonal quality in that it brings with it (or facilitates) fantasies in which our wishes regarding relationship with another can be fulfilled. Because of this interpersonal parameter, sex often invites the expression and attempted resolution of nonsexual struggles around polarities of personal relationship. These include dominance and submission. parenting and dependency, persecuting and playing victim, power and helplessness, and tenderness and violence.

The fourth parameter of sexuality, that which pivots the *dependable-expendable-interpersonal* qualities full tilt into the arena, is its *vulnerability* to subtle shifts of mood, attitude, and behavior in the self and in the partner. Men and women are so easily "turned on" and "turned off" by a gesture, a word, a facial expression that sexual interplay becomes a most tempting battleground on which to carry on the nuances of unresolved longings and resentments, feelings that arose in other human contexts that were not primarily sexual.

Willfulness, stubbornness, spite, and other petty insistences of maintaining the illusion of being in control of that which we cannot control, run rampant in the relationship between the sexes. The unwillingness to be vulnerable, to be helpless, to give up control, to trust, is deployed in a mad attempt either to get one's own way, or failing that, at least to make sure that the partner does not get his (her) own way. *Getting our own way*, that which Dame Alice says is what women want most, is, God help us, as often what men want most for themselves as well.

5. Tale of a Power Trip

When first we meet Macbeth,[1] he is a brave and loyal commanding general in the service of King Duncan of Scotland, fresh from victory in battle in the King's name. Satisfied to serve, he is pledged to support Duncan's reign, both as "his kinsman and his subject."[2]

Told by three witches that his future holds promise of promotion, that someday he even "shalt be king hereafter," his latent hunger for power is aroused. Once content to serve those in power, he now begins to know the "black and deep desires" for greatness, the "vaulted ambition" for a position above other men. He suddenly sees anyone who stands between him and his ascendance to the throne as "a step on which I must fall down or else o'erleap, for in my way it lies."[3] His power trip has begun.

Though troubled by uncertainties and indecision, with the support of the ruthless ambition of his "dearest partner of greatness,"[4] Lady Macbeth, he goes on to kill the King, putting the blame onto others. His wife, at each point, spurs him on to do whatever is required to achieve power and greatness. He would not have murdered his liege, had she not mocked and taunted him "to be the same in thine own act and valor as thou art in desire."[5]

Power trips often figure centrally in the struggles of the psychotherapy patient/pilgrim as well. The ironic difference is that these patients have most often been trapped into seeking an illusory form of power, one which ultimately renders them powerless. It is not the proverbial political power which "corrupts absolutely" that does them in. Their search has more in common

with Macbeth's obsessively hungry ambition. It is not
the power he wields, but rather the demonically soul-
absorbing longings for ascendance that eat away at
Macbeth's character.

Like Macbeth, the neurotic has been part of a family
conspiracy, but his power plays lack the substance of
Macbeth's violent acts with their realpolitik consequences. The metaphor of the matador may help to
make the differences clearer. Think of Macbeth as a
bullfighter, risking his life in the arena. Except for the
support of his picador (Lady Macbeth), he has only
his relentless determination, the brilliance of his cape
work, and the power of his sword to go in over the
horns of the bull at the moment of truth. For the
neurotic it is almost the same—stubborn determination,
family support, brilliantly distracting flairs of the cape,
and keen sword at the ready for the kill. Only one difference: in the arena of the neurotic, there is no bull!

The psychotherapy patient is likely then to be struggling with the *illusion of interpersonal power,* the fantasy of having power over other people's feelings, an
ironic mock potency that places the "master" in bondage, while giving sovereignty to the alleged "victim."

One instance of this cruel and foolish illusion of interpersonal power is that of the young son's mistaken
idea that he can emerge ascendant in the family triad.
Woe betide the boy who makes the mistake of believing that he has won the Oedipal struggle! Mother may
insist that he will become a better man than father ever
was, indeed that he is already more thoughtful, more
considerate, more responsible, and braver than his
worthless old man. Father may conspire to support
the illusion by seeming to be ready to turn over the
care and feeding of mother to the young contender.
This parental collusion misleads the young prince into
believing that his power has been legitimatized.

Only gradually does the boy discover that his position is more a matter of awesome responsibilities than
of freedom and privilege. In trying to learn how to become a man, without having a strong father who will

show him the way, the boy is in the position of having to invent himself. He must become mother's little man without having had a chance to live out the protected dependency of being a little boy. The coronation is a fake. He has been taken.

The destructive effects of the underlying fraud become clear when, as a man, he enters therapy. He feels driven, and yet he somehow never accomplishes enough. He is weary, but he feels guilty whenever he takes time out to rest from his resented obligatory striving. As he tells his tale, he comes to realize that his place in the family was not that of potentate, but of pawn. Not only was he not really the central power, but instead he was a willing dupe. Doubly robbed both of mother's nurturant caretaking and of father's strong protection and model for growth, the prince has been no more than a patsy.

His parents originally came together because of their interest in each other. They made love out of their desire for that shared intimacy. They were not thinking about him at the time when he was conceived. They went on being intimate and running the family together all during his figurehead reign. And now that he is grown, and living elsewhere, carrying the burden of his childhood power-illusions into his adult work and into his own marriage, they remain together. Their marriage continues in his absence. Mother is making it without her dauphin, and father is still secretly in charge.

The illusion of power led the son to work when he should have played. It mediated his taking care of the mother at a time when she should have been taking care of him. And too, it cost him the strengthening support of a visibly assertive father.

Macbeth, of course, also ended up paying too dearly for the brief opportunity to see himself as greater than other men, as sufficient unto himself, and as invulnerable to their power. Certainly he was done in by his own ambition, but others colluded in his ultimate downfall. The three witches offered ambiguous prophecies of his triumphs, which Macbeth seized upon as assurances that his power would be secure, that he was impervious to the retaliatory power of others. His cruelly ambitious wife urged him on toward deception and murder, only to fall from his side soon afterwards, lost in guilt, dying of despair. His character crumbled, as he was driven to worse and worse crimes in order to maintain his uncertain hold on the mercurial omnipotence that cost him his integrity, his freedom, and, finally, his life.

One way or another, power over others always turns out to be a costly burden. A sense of one's own strength, and freedom to do with it what you will, brings with it a feeling of expansiveness, of exultation. If the realm in which this power is to be realized is turned toward the creative possibilities of the self, then the excitement and joy become possible. But, if this freedom is experienced as *power over others,* both parties will be trapped. It does not matter whether the power is used benevolently or for exploitation, the result is the same. If I see other adults as weaker than I am in our personal relationships, it does not matter whether they volunteer to be wards whom I must protect or victims whom I am to exploit. If I conspire with them to the illusion of either sort of power, whether benign or malevolent, we will both be trapped in a symbiotic bargain. My sense of power over others will limit my freedom to live out my wishes for myself. Either I will be obligated to take care of my wards, or I will have to waste myself in putting down mutinous serfs and guarding against victims who would retaliate.

This paradox arises for some people in their earliest years. As children, they are powerless. They need care. Kids are entitled. For a child to be able first to survive and then to grow toward being a happy, creatively self-fulfilling adult, he must be taken care of by his parents. His physical needs for food, warmth, and protection from injury are the base line. But too, he must be provided with situations that support his maturation, with encouragement to do those things for which he is ready, and with parental structuring that does not ask him to take on difficult activities too early.

The most insidious of the premature responsibilities that may be foisted onto some children is the expectation that the child is somehow supposed to take care of his parents, rather than the other way around. Parents who were themselves raised with too little attention given to their own early feelings, if they have not worked out the resulting emotional problems in subsequent years, often look forward to having children of their own so that the children will make *them* happy.

I remember one such overburdened child who as an adult came to me for therapy with the complaint that she was chronically depressed and intermittently panicky about the burdens and responsibilities of her job. As a small child she had lost her father, and her refusing-to-grow-up petulant mother insisted that Phyllis make up to her for the frustration of widowhood, by being the best at everything she tried, by making mother proud of her.

For a long time Phyllis was sustained by the feeling that she was very important, that she had the power (along with the attendant obligation) to relieve mother's dreary existence. She rarely played or did things just for herself. Instead, she gave herself over to excelling in school, to keeping house for her beleaguered working mother, to becoming an outstanding student of music and dance, and to taking care of her younger sister.

At first, when she experienced something as being too hard for her, when she felt confused, or when she suffered some of the disappointments all children encounter, she turned to mother for comfort. The false sense of importance to a mother whom she had the power of making happy led her to feel that she should expect warmth and sympathy from this woman who surely loved her. But whenever she made the mistake of coming to mother with her troubles, mother met Phyllis's tears with her own, explaining that her daughter's

well-being was so important to her that she could not
stand to see her unhappy. Each time the result was the
same. Phyllis came to her, crying out for understanding, only to end up having to comfort mother instead.

Eventually, Phyllis learned to be a super-competent
big girl, rather than bother poor mother. She only
felt good about herself when she was accomplishing
something that she imagined would make mother proud
of her. She grew up to be a bright, attractive woman
and was able to earn graduate degrees, become a respected professional in her field, and receive an appointment to run an important government project. By
the time she came to see me she was having trouble
getting up each morning to go to work, felt (without
objective evidence) that her job was so difficult for her
that for the first time she would fail and let everyone
down. She also found herself crying more and more
often, but she didn't want to bother me with that because there was no good reason for her tears. One
more thing. She had a lovely, mad desire to scrap the
whole thing and become a go-go dancer.

She hoped that I would help her to get over that
playful wish, because if she failed professionally she
would make her husband unhappy, as well as letting
down all the people at work who depended on her.

From the time of our very first meeting, I found
Phyllis to be a delightfully appealing human being (except when she was trying to impress me with how
much she was willing to do to make me happy). She
had no control over the things about her that I like
best: her warmth, her spontaneity, her vulnerability,
and the depth of feeling she showed when she was not
being self-conscious. I let her know in many ways that
I didn't care at all whether she stayed on with the
government to make a great success of the project she
was running, or if instead she chose to run off to the
mischievously mindless fun of being a go-go dancer.
My only interest was in helping her to find some
happiness that would be just for herself, regardless of

whether or not her friends and family were pleased or upset by how she ran her life.

Again and again, she read her own pain and disapproval into my reactions and frantically tried to gear her own behavior to keeping me happy. Only a bit at a time did she come to realize that though I liked her, I did not need her, no more than did any of the other people whom she felt she had to protect from the illusory abuse of her fantasied power over them. Her magical fantasy died hard, because she got so much satisfaction out of the mirage of being in charge of everyone else's well-being. But after a while, she began to experience the new reality of each person as being as strong and as weak as anyone else. Slowly, she learned that each of us grown-ups had as much and as little power as the other, and that we had best learn to take care of ourselves. If someone else didn't like it, that was his problem.

Power illusions such as the one Phyllis lived out are always the result of an early two-party contract. One of the signers is a person who feels that he must take care of others, who comes to experience the desires for his own happiness as injurious to the feelings of someone else. It is as if there was only a certain amount of happiness to go round. The accomplice in this bad bargain is a centrally important person in his life (perhaps first a parent, then later a spouse), another deluded individual, but this time with a reciprocal power illusion. The party of the second part is one who insists that his own welfare depends on how the empowered first party lives his own life. For each person who volunteers to live the life of a tool, lest he turn out to be a knife, there is another who threatens to become a wound.

It is my very strong impression that in such bargains, the victim is far more dangerous than the powerful, responsibility-burdened caretaker. Beware the helplessness gambit of the chronic victim! Some people typically get out from under their own responsibilities in difficult situations (in which they would otherwise have to take care of themselves) by acting helpless and weak in order to invite others to do for them. If the other person does not respond, then he is accused of being cruel and unfeeling. But should he arrogantly take on the role of caretaker, then the helpless one will soon hold him in contempt as being a weak fool, and what he offers will be returned as somehow not good enough. In the long run, the helper is made to feel helpless. Finally the victim is in the power position (though he has won nothing but the degrading imposition of his will by playing through weakness, or failing that, he settles for the spiteful sense of having been able to keep the other from having had his way).

When such a helpless victim seeks my guidance as a psychotherapist, it soon becomes clear that he will do nothing to clear up the mess of his own life and that, because I am supposed to be stronger, I am to do it for him. Whenever I yield to the temptation to try to help, it turns out that I don't really understand what is needed, that I come too late and with too little. As I begin to unhook, to be available without trying to take care of such a patient, I am accused of being callous, devoid of human compassion. My amusement makes things even hairier, and sometimes the patient will quit, whiningly adding my name to the list of therapists who let him down. In some cases, the patient continues in treatment, hanging around to complain about getting nowhere. I reinforce his despair, agreeing that he probably will be just this unhappy all of his life, that not all stories have happy endings. If the patient can mobilize his rage at me for not caring (at his parents for keeping him a helpless pawn to their degrading caretaking), then he may become willing to fight for his life, to struggle for earned happiness. With that I will gladly help him.

Sometimes it seems to me that in this absurdly random life, there is some inherent justice in the outcome of personal relationships. In the long run, we get no more than we have been willing to risk giving. We get to keep no more than we earn by our own efforts. In a way, we each get what we deserve. Everyone is entitled to keep as much garbage as he is willing to put out or to put up with.

Phyllis's apparent concern for my feelings, her wish to be the good patient so that I would be happy with her, was by no means an expression of love, or even of good will. She resented coming to therapy, having to work to pay me, as well as committing herself to get down to business each session. Periodically this resentment would be expressed in a petulant period of nonproductive sulking or in acting out between sessions of bad girl behavior. To see how much crap I would put up with, periodically she spat out an abusive tirade at what she experienced as my lack of appreciation of her efforts on my behalf.

She seemed for a time to be so preoccupied with accomplishing something to please me so that I would accept her, that she absolutely could not comprehend that I liked her very much just the way she was. (If she wanted to change something in herself for her own best interests, I would be willing to help, but I had no personal need for her to change at all.) It was far more frightening for her to accept the way I valued her as a gift, a stroke of grace over which she had no control, than to struggle to find some way to sing for her supper, to purchase acceptance (or at least to rent it). That way, at least, she could maintain the illusion that she had power over my happiness (as well as the option of rescinding it if need be).

As she told her tale, we talked some about what sort of little girl she had been. I expressed curiosity about that point in her growing up at which she had decided that she was not sufficient, at what point she had felt the need to take on the responsibility of becoming someone that mother could be proud of.

Phyllis's recounting reminded me of the lines in the diaries of Anaïs Nin that expressed equivalent self-determination. Anaïs writes:

If my father left, it must be that he did not love me,
and if he did not [love me], it must have been because
I was not lovable. I was going to interest him in other
ways. I was going to become interesting. And I grew
in depth through sadness and self-doubt. As a courtesan, at the age of nine, I had already experienced
failure so I must try other ways to interest men.[6]

Though I will not discuss them here, Phyllis's go-go
girl aspirations also contained some similar elements.

It is always a touching experience to go with a patient back far enough in the retelling of her own tale
to approach that point at which she can once more
see herself as too young to be reproached. In an ex-
ploration such as this, the patient reaches a place of
bewildering delight with herself (or himself) when she
realizes that there was a time when she was all right,
just the way she was, just being herself. Usually, this
point is established as a recollection of what she must
have been like at the age of two or three. Instinctively,
we all find toddlers lovable and appealing (otherwise
the species would have become extinct, with no young
ones surviving without these caring responses that their
very nature evokes in parenting adults). Even the most
neurotically self-deprecating adult cannot maintain the
absurd image that she was once inadequate at being a
baby. It would be like trying to maintain the image of
a kitten who did not know how to be a kitten.

The warming recognition of herself as a lovable
child often generates many real memories of what she
looked like, how she acted, and how appealing people
outside of the family sometimes found her to be. It is
at this point that the patient's bitterness starts to
emerge, as she begins to realize that if she has lost
her delight with the child she once was, it is because
others misled her. They taught her that she was somehow not pleasing enough. Through parental expressions
of dissatisfaction and unhappiness, she learned that
there *must* be something wrong with her.

Of course, one other hypothetical alternative would

have been for the child to decide that since she was fine the way she was, there must have been something terribly wrong with her parents. But children need at least the continuing *hope* that their parents may come to love them. To decide that these crazy parents will never love her, no matter what she does, no matter whom she becomes, would leave a child buried in a depth of despair in which she would surely suffocate and die.

The child's only experienced option is to decide that she has made her parents unhappy, and that perhaps there is some way in which she could change that would make them happy once more. At this point of decision, the terrifying helplessness of the child's situation gives way to the promise of power. If she has indeed made them unhappy (no matter how awful that feels), then she *does* matter, she *is* important to them. Now begins the desperate search for cues in parental expression that suggest how this power might be developed, just what it is the child might be able to do to set things right.

In the course of the retelling of her tale, she recognizes that she bought her parents' crazy devaluation of her worth; then comes a time of confusion and of a struggle to change what cannot be changed. Then slowly, unevenly, in fragments, bits and pieces, the amalgam of destructive bitterness may give way to its component rage and grief. Usually the anger breaks loose first in the form of recriminations against the unfairness of those who should have loved her. She demands to know why this happened to her. When I tell her that there is no reason, her anger is spat out at me.

But as she begins to see that her tragedy is the random expression of being born into the wrong house, the anger gives way to the wailing over what might have been. Any child born into that family, at that time, would have been as little appreciated. The actuarial conditions that might have influenced her fate include such factors as what sex the child turns out to be, her place in the birth order of the siblings (and how it relates to the parents' places in their own early families), the stage of the marriage at which she was born, the family's economic situation, and so on. Her destiny did not have anything to do with what sort of child she really was. Had she been born to the family next door, she might have been valued and enjoyed for the sort of lovely little girl she once was.

What a waste of her life to spend herself trying to be something good enough for mother, when she was already good enough. Nothing could ever be good enough to finally satisfy such a mother. If she can face what a fool she has been to have tried and tried to transform her vitality into a power that would make this insatiable mother happy, she may then be able to reclaim her power for herself. She never had any real power over mother, or over the feelings of anyone else. Her only real power lies in taking charge of her own life, enjoying being who she is, and making her life as meaningful as she can *for herself,* whatever others may or may not expect of her.

But the past cannot be buried without the pain of mourning. She must try to face just how really bad she feels, and how helplessly stuck she is with her own tale. Instead of trying to muster the power to be perfect enough to satisfy others, of feeling the fraudulent responsibility of being seemingly dangerous to the happiness of others, all she can do is to begin more and more to take the chance of letting herself be known. She must reveal her imperfect, inconsistent, good/bad, weak/strong, all-too-human self to the rest of us, so that we may get to know her and become known to her. If some don't love her, no doubt others will. In any case, no one can take another's place. You win some, you lose some, and your losses are never made up to you. She will simply have to do without; like it or not, she must face her losses and her helplessness to undo them. She

must weep, and mourn, and grieve them through. [She] . . . must unhook from the past to make room for the present. In burying the parents of childhood, [she] . . . must make do with the rest of the world minus two. Not such a bad trade after all.[7]

The illusion of power over the feelings of others is a deadly chimera. We, none of us, are any stronger than any other grown-up. And certainly, we were each more vulnerable, more helpless, and more dependent as children than the parents who misled those of us who took on more than we were really ready to handle.

But that part is done now, that time when my own personal world was divided into the weak and the powerful. I, for one, have learned half the lesson well. I can see through the apparent power of others. There are few people in my life now who have the real political power to impose close-quarter tyranny on my actions. I will not, of course, stand toe-to-toe with a club-wielding policeman, but the mock ferocity of most other people no longer intimidates me.

I've really got it straight in my head that no one is any bigger than I am. It's the other part that I can still sometimes get hung up on. I still occasionally insist on getting caught up in the illusion that some people (aside from little kids) are smaller, weaker, or more vulnerable than I am. At my worst moments, I am still tempted to the arrogant presumption that I can victimize other people, lesser beings whose fragile feelings I should somehow be taking care of. Lord protect me from the so-called "victims"!

6. Tale of a Mad Knight

I prefer the madness of Don Quixote to the sanity of most other men. Cervante's Knight of the Rueful Countenance, Don Quixote de la Mancha,[1] is alleged to have become deluded by the brain-addling effects of his continued immersion in the reading of chivalric tales of "enchantments, knightly encounters, battles, challenges, wounds, . . . love and its torments, and all sorts of impossible things."[2]

Ignoring the staid dissuasions of family and friends, this quiet, middle-aged, country-village gentleman gave way to his madness and decided to sally forth to spend the remainder of his life as a knight-errant. In order to serve God and country, as well as to win honor for himself, he set out in an ill-fitting suit of rusty second-hand, makeshift armor, astride a tired hack of a horse to whom he assigned the weighty name of Rocinante. He set out to roam the world (of rural seventeenth-century Spain) on an adventurous quest to set right whatever wrongs he might encounter, in the name of social justice and for the attainment of personal glory.

Though he exaggerated his own importance, had a distorted view of what he encountered, and overestimated his chances of setting things to rights, the world into which he sallied forth was really (like our own) unjust. Perhaps it demands such a holy fool as Don Quixote to take the evil of the world seriously enough and to imagine himself sufficiently adequate to be willing to dedicate his life to improving the suffering lot of others. It takes "a Gothic Christ, torn by modern anguish to face the sufferings of this absurd world; a ridiculous Christ of our own neighborhood, created by a sorrowful imagination which [has] lost its innocence and its will and is striving to replace them."[8]

Attempts at social change are after all usually left to the youthful idealists, while older cynics wait for young fools to outgrow their folly. I remember well some of my own early adventures as a young psychologist. My first job was on the staff of a dead-end, monolithic warehouse for the insane known as a State Mental Hospital. My innocence kept me from realizing that efforts to help patients in such a tragic/comic setting were hopelessly doomed to failure. As yet unbattered, my fresh personal commitment, naïvely boundless enthusiasm, and exaggerated self-confidence allowed me to accomplish impossible feats, to do what could not be done. I spent hours talking to hopelessly unresponsive, forgotten, catatonic men and women until eventually, in some, a spark of life returned to long-empty eyes. Only after age and experience made me more "realistic" did I achieve professional sanity, so that I was no longer able to be of any help to those poor captive souls.

Needing a fair lady to whom he may dedicate his quest, Don Quixote selected a lovely local farm girl with whom he had been secretly infatuated as the princess of his mad dreams. He resolved to call her Dulcinea del Toboso, a name worthy of the royal station to which he had elevated her. Though this too seems a matter of insane fancy, his fantasy dedication of courtly love seems to me no more crazy than the wonderfully bewildering experience, which we have all been through (and some more than once), the phenomenon that we call "falling in love." It may even be that "imagination has created all [of] the most perfect ladies [and gentlemen and that] . . . he who sees his lady just as she is is no lover worthy of the name."[4]

It is of course possible to describe Reality reductively as *nothing but* this or that. What woman, for the cynically hyper-realistic man, is any more than a rag, a bone, and a hank of hair? The human body can be reduced to its chemical components enmeshed in a set of physical interactions, but that which is most human is lost in the analyzed ashes. It is an improverished chemical baggage who lives in a world to which he will not bring vitality and meaning. Life is very dull for those too timid, too unimaginative, too sane to bring to it a sense of personal style, of individual purpose, of color, verve, fun, and excitement. Don Quixote's Quest, the personal pilgrimage of his mad life, was to live in *"the world as it* is traversed by *man as he ought to be."*[5] If this be the wine of madness, then I say: "Come fill my cup."

It greatly upset the other members of Don Quixote's family and his community to learn that he had chosen to believe in himself. They were contemptuous of his wish to follow his dream. They did not connect the inception of the Knight's madness with the deadly drabness of his living amidst their pietism. His prissy niece, his know-what's-best-for-everyone housekeeper, his dull barber, and the pompous village-priest, all knew that it was his dangerous books that had filled Don Quixote's failing mind with foolish ideas and so made him crazy.

Their household reminds me of the families from which young schizophrenics sometimes emerge. Such families often give the appearance of hyper-normal stability and moralistic goodness. What actually goes on is that they have developed an elaborately subtle system of cues to warn any member should he be about to do something spontaneous, something that would topple the precarious family balance and expose the hypocrisy of their over-controlled pseudo-stability.

I remember one couple who for years had used their daughter's academic achievements both as proof of what a constructive family life they had and as a focus for the appearance of closeness that masked their dread of real intimacy. In late adolescence the girl's growing interest in sex threatened the family with her establishing an intimate relationship with someone outside of their system of control. Parental religious preoccupation quickened, and soon they were surprised and upset to find that their daughter (the identified patient) had become crazy, developing hallucinatory visions to support the delusion that she was to be the reincarnation of the Virgin Mary.

At first the family was "resigned" to having to take care of their crazy child for the rest of her (their) life. They had no intention of having her hospitalized, and only sought treatment because her confusion began interfering with her schoolwork. In a therapy group of such families, and with some individual support, after a while the crazy daughter began to manifest new nonfamilial sanity in the form of questioning her own delusional experiences, thinking of quitting school to get a job, and hoping to move out on her own. At this point, father spoke out against the destructively secular influence of psychotherapy, begging his daughter not to discard her "visions," because "in matters of the spirit, who are we to judge?"

In Don Quixote's case, the auspicious community of the wise and the sane took it upon themselves to judge his books and to burn them. Cervantes's chilling parody of the Spanish Inquisition is echoed by our own contemporary experiences with forces of Law and Order and by the current and recent Administration's attempts to protect us from dangerous ideas and information, *for our own good*.

In a subtler way, the protective efforts of the self-appointed sane influence the whole field of psychiatry and psychology. The clinical diagnosis of psychopathology is too often a form of social control. If other people make *us* nervous by the foreignness of their queer talk and odd behavior, we give *them* tranquilizing drugs, lock *them* away in custodial institutions.

I once witnessed an ironically enlightening instance of the cultural definition of insanity, and of the power politics of psychiatric social control. At the time when I was on the staff of a New Jersey State Mental Hospital, a strange man appeared on a street corner in Trenton, wearing a long white sheet and quietly muttering "gibberish." His very presence threatened the certitude of sanity of the community at large. Fortunately, for the sheeted man's own good, a policeman was called by some saner citizen. So it was that this poor man was able to be brought under the protective lock-and-key of his local Asylum.

His efforts to explain his strange behavior were offered in vain, since it was clear that he was a loony, or to be more scientific, he was diagnosed into that catch-all garbage can of a syndrome known as Schizophrenia, Chronic Undifferentiated Type. It would have been difficult for anyone to acquit himself well in that diagnostic staff situation, since the patient was assumed to be crazy until proven sane, unrepresented by counsel, and not even told that anything he said could be used against him.

One further limitation was in play, accruing epiphenomenally from the sociology of American medicine. Foreign-trained physicians are not allowed to practice medicine in this country until they have demonstrated competence both in English and in medicine. So far, so good. However, in the absence of such proven competence, they are permitted to work as resident psychiatrists in state mental institutions. I have seen irascible (but otherwise normal) citizens diagnosed as confused psychotics, adjudged incompetent, and denied their civil rights and their freedom on the basis of their inability to understand the incompetent mouthings of ill-trained resident psychiatrists whose own command of English was so limited that I could not understand them either.

Fortunately, for the white-sheeted, gibberish-muttering patient in question, the hospital Visitors' Day began the very next morning. Evidently he had called home and made his plight known. That morning twenty other people wearing white sheets arrived at the hospital. Equally strangely clad, they were also equivalently incomprehensible to the psychiatric staff. It turned out (to the resident psychiatrist's amusement) that these men and women were all members of the same small rural church sect, a religious group who defined their identity in part by clothing themselves in the purity of white cloth, and by being divinely inspired to talk in tongues. The psychiatrist in this case, being a practicing Roman Catholic (who weekly ate and drank the body and the blood of Jesus Christ) thought they were a queer bunch indeed. Heaven help him should he ever wander into a community in which his own religious affiliations would be equally obscure. The patient was released that afternoon. One such man is a lunatic. Twenty constitute an acceptable and sane community.

Don Quixote's madness and his loss of contact with reality are played off against the down-to-earth sanity of Sancho Panza, a local peasant whom he has convinced to accompany him as his squire. Sancho is committed to a common-sense approach, believing only what he can see with his own eyes. Yet he goes along with Don Quixote's mad sallies into the illusion of adventure, because Sancho in his so-called sanity is driven by greed. He wishes to gain worldly power, to become the governor of an island whose sovereignty Don Quixote promises him as a reward for service. Again and again, Sancho kids himself that his knight knows what he is about, his self-deception guided by his "sane" insistence on the acquisition of power.

Time after time, Sancho is unnerved by Don Quixote's impulsive challenging and attacking of swineherds, mule drivers, and innkeepers whom he mistakes for enchanters, evil knights, and lords of the manor. Yet each time Sancho endures what he must (with expedient cowardice in the face of fire) in the search for his own impossible dream. How meager and empty are the squire's desires for petty officialdom when compared with his knight's mad wish to right the wrongs of this world.

Perhaps the most famous of their escapades is what is now commonly referred to as quixotic fighting with windmills. Arriving on a great plain, the adventurers see thirty or forty windmills which Don Quixote mistakes for "lawless giants."[6] Sancho cannot convince him that their turning wings are not mighty arms. Don

Quixote charges to do battle with these giants, is un-
seated by the turning of the giant's arm, and ends up
badly battered, on the ground, with broken lance. But,
consider for a moment what it took for him to do battle with these illusory forces of evil. After all, "who
doubts that the courage to face giants is both more ad-
mirable and more rare than the ability to recognize a
fulling mill when one hears it?"[7] Distorted views of the
world do not always constitute corruption of the purpose of one's quest.

I remember my concern for social justice when my
own life was brushed by the dark wing of madness.
Following a near-catastrophic ordeal of intra-cranial
surgery, an adverse response to the drugs I had been
given, and a disorienting experience of slipping back
and forth between sleep and pain under the unwavering
overhead lights of the intensive care unit, I was crazy
for several days afterward.

To begin with, I was confused, terrified, could not
understand, and did not know if it would ever end. A
bad trip. I was sure they were trying to hurt me. They
had put some device into my nose; it hurt and so I
pulled it out. It was bloody, and then I was sure they
were trying to kill me. Because I interfered with their
efforts, they tied down my hands (later I learned that
this was done with gauze, but then I thought I had
been chained). I felt helpless, enraged, humiliated. I
tried to punch one of the nurses in the face. In retro-
spect, I realize that I must have been a pain in the ass
to them, that they continued to try to help, and that I
must have correctly read the resentment behind their
attempts to reassure me that they really wanted to help
me. But I was too smart for them. I knew. I became
more and more cunning in tricking them into removing some of the more tortuous breathing devices
they had put on me.

Some of my perceptions became more elaborate but
not more clear. The hospital seemed somehow anti-
Semitic and my persecution a part of that. Some of

the equipment seemed Jewish and all right, but some
of it seemed Christian and worried me. Also, though I
wanted to sleep, I visualized this as some sort of
"tableau" being set up so that as I slept, the video-tape
footage of my sleeping would be used as comic relief
in whatever kind of T.V. show this was that they were
putting on. At last, I recognized my wife at my bedside
. . . I told her to get an investigating committee from
the American Civil Liberties Union to check on their
tying my hands without due process.[8]

During the painful weeks that followed, as I was
struggling to make sense of this psychotic episode, I
received an answering letter from a loving friend. This
lovely man is a Jungian psychiatrist out on the West
Coast, and here is what he wrote to me about the sanity
of my craziness:

> How marvelously and strangely correct that you would
> encounter one of your demons within the cavern that
> houses the possession which your race [the Jews] and
> our society values most highly, the intellect. . . . You
> found yourself in a strange land, a land somehow de-
> termined by your racial forebearers. That strange and
> dangerous land which you identify as your psychosis
> but is simply a naturally existing deeper layer of un-
> conscious which is always there but rarely experienced
> directly by the conscious human being. You found
> only one source that could be trusted to identify you
> as yourself and who remained unquestionably herself.
> [He refers here to my wife.]

> I felt great empathy with you when I read . . . of your
> fear of being attended to by a contemporary repre-
> sentative of the mental hospital. [Some patients] have
> been almost destroyed by the "help" they receive from
> well-trained, well-intentioned, well-experienced psy-
> chiatrists. Fortunately, as in your own experience, the
> basic health of the individual is usually stronger than
> the well-intentioned or inadvertently applied medicine.

> In your delusion, you knew the true basis for your
> persecution, namely your faith. . . . I know how diffi-

cult it is to fight a religious war without the benefit of
recognized deities. It seems evident to me that the
enemy was clearly identified by you both in your more
accustomed conscious state and in your deeply unconscious state as being the impersonalizing forces that
you encountered. You even tried to give some life-
meaning to the impersonalizing machines which were
being used on your body . . . by identifying them as
machines of one faith or another. . . . The truest
statement of your situation was that if you permitted
yourself to lapse into the totally unconscious state of
sleep, in your unconsciousness, your very condition as
a human being would be used to hold you up to
ridicule and abuse.[9]

I do not mean to suggest, by all of the foregoing discussion of the value of madness, that craziness as such
is a good thing. Rather, I wish to point out that in a
world in which true madness masquerades as sanity,
creative struggles against the ongoing myths will seem
eccentric and will be labeled as "crazy" by the challenged establishment in power. We who are sane know
that our technology will save us, that war is inevitable,
that poverty and hunger of a few of the undeserving
poor are necessary to the well-being of the many. These
drug-crazy, Commie-fag-hippies who talk about making love instead of war, who want to live on communes
without indoor plumbing, who want to make their own
rules, these kids have to be stopped. Lock 'em up, punish them, straighten them out, before they end up destroying all the ways that the good Lord has intended
us to live.

Of course, being crazy can instead be a stubborn
expression of self-destructive willfulness. There appear
to be many people who choose to go crazy (or become
alcoholics, addicts, criminals, suicides) rather than have
to bear the pain and ambiguity of a life situation that
they have decided that they cannot stand. With such
patients, I try to make clear that I cannot prevent their
going mad, but that I will not follow their madcap
course from home to hospital and back. They may

have any crazy feelings and ideas they wish, but in their community they have to act *as if* they were sane, if they want me to accompany them on their pilgrimage. The irresponsible act of going crazy, in order not to have to face up to the mess they have created in their own lives, is not one to which I wish to be an accomplice.

During my own above-described hospitalization, I was fortunate enough to have been too weak physically to have acted out all of my madness. As a result, I survived, and I believe that I learned a valuable lesson. At one point, just after the operation and just before my psychotic episode, my breathing had stopped several times and my life was in jeopardy. The hospital's respiration team had forced rubber tubing down into my throat to pump the fluids out of my lungs. Then the nurse tied an oxygen mask over my face. The cold gas felt like fire in the rawness of my throat.

Weakly, I signaled the nurse to come to my bedside. She removed the mask for a moment to find out what was the matter. I gasped: "The mask, take it off. I can't stand it." She answered with quiet confidence: "Yes, you can!" She put the oxygen mask back on and saved my life.

My madness, it seems to me, followed this exchange. Though conditioned by the physiological trauma of brain surgery, it was also an ambiguous conglomerate of crazy flight from the helplessness, which I did not want to face, and a desperate attempt to maintain my personal integrity in a world that made no sense. It was good and bad, filled for me with what may always remain insoluble contradictions. It was what it was. Writing about it seems to help some.

At the end of a series of colorfully zany misadventures, Don Quixote also achieved sanity. On his deathbed he had to endure the moralistic admonishment of his deadly sane housekeeper: "Stay at home, attend to your affairs, go often to confession, be charitable to the poor." Such is the lesson of sane virtue, "but a man may have to go through hell to learn it."[10] And so, safe from any further threat of madness, Don Quixote died "having gained his reason and lost his reasons for living."[11]

It should be clear to the reader who has accompanied me through the labyrinth of this chapter that I do not feel that I have any once-and-for-all clear understanding of madness. Sometimes it seems like it is the only way to travel in a dully sane and destructively stable world. In other instances it seems to me to be an irresponsibly willful cop-out. And in any given situation, it may seem like some of each. My hope would not be to totally avoid madness, but rather to hold out against that face of it that turns me away from the courage I need in the presence of threat, away from Hemingway's "grace under pressure." As for its other face, I value my own craziness and the creative places it can take me, free of the constraints of pedestrian Reason and unimaginative predictability.

Let me describe one instance in which I felt that encouraging the craziness of another was a way of helping him along the way of his pilgrimage.

Dan was an intellectual warrior, a super-competent, though somewhat over-gunned, young man. He leaned heavily on Reason to make his way, working at all he did with clarity of purpose, sharpness of intent, and an air of weariness born of cognitive overexertion. In therapy, he told his tale in a well-organized fashion, presenting a careful self-analysis, a report replete with answers, but empty of solutions. I responded by being confounded by his irrelevant "insights" and fatigued by his continued efforts to be rational. And too, I let him know that the blunt sanity of his explanations was beginning to confuse me, and the only thing that made me feel we might be getting somewhere was my own growing confusion.

His exasperation over our "lack of communication" and the growing deterioration of his illusion of clarity led Dan to redouble his efforts to master the situation. Of course, it got worse and worse. Then one day he came in upset, but triumphant, to report a dream which explained to him why he was getting so irritated with me.

"I dreamed last night that I was at sea, aboard a battleship. I couldn't see you, but I sensed that you were out there somewhere beyond the horizon. It was awful! My ship was falling apart. The seams were buckling, and sections of the steel armor plate were breaking loose and dropping off into the water. Everything was crumbling. I began to get panicky because I knew the ship would surely sink. As soon as I woke up, I realized that the dream was about what's going on in therapy. The more I talk with you, the more I feel like *I'm* coming apart at the seams. What the hell are you trying to do to me anyway, drive me crazy?"

Of course, I was trying to drive him crazy, and I told him that this was a fine dream, that I really liked it, assuring him that the only reason that it bothered *him* was because he thought he understood it. Even more disgusted, he countered: "All right, if you're so smart, you explain it!" I pointed out that dreams can be understood, but they cannot be "explained." If he wanted to really understand his own dream, he would have to re-experience it by letting himself go crazy enough to become the sea, instead of restricting his place to the helm of that crumbling toy boat.

For a moment, he looked at me as though he couldn't get too angry because *I* was surely mad. Then, as if to indulge me, he sat quietly with his eyes closed for a few minutes, trying to let himself get hold of the nonsense of being the sea. When he finally opened his eyes, they were wide with wonder. His usual penetrating gaze was gone, his expression transformed. His face and voice were animated in a new way, and the muscles of his strong, tense jaw seemed relaxed for the first time.

It was difficult for him to bring his usual precision to the description of the experience he had just had. "It's all so different," he said. "When I'm the sea, it's as though I have no boundaries. I move so easily, and feel so free of struggle. And then I could see that even if the ship fell apart and went under, it would just sink into the water, and rust away to become part of the sea. It's as though nothing is ever really lost, so there's no problem, nothing that has to be defended."

There was much work yet to be done in therapy. But after his experience of being the sea, Dan was more often undefended and spontaneous. Sometimes when he felt uptight, ready to struggle for control of a situation, he remembered that he could go crazy and let himself be the sea, and his need to do battle would run out like the tide.

7. Tale of a Descent into Hell

At Easter time, in the Year of Our Lord 1300, the Florentine poet Dante Alighieri descended into the Inferno of Hell.[1]

Some say that his tale is mainly a medium for exposing the social and political evils of his time. Others insist that Dante represents Mankind, that human life itself is the journey, and that "Hell is the death which must precede rebirth."[2] It is also possible to view his trip as taking place in inner space, as a descent into the pit of his own soul, showing that the sinful soul itself is Hell.

I agree with Eliot, that "the aim of the poet is to state a vision . . . [and that] Dante, more than any other poet, has succeeded in dealing with his philosophy, not as a theory . . . or as his comment or reflection, but in terms of something *perceived*."[3] Open yourself to listening to his tale, if you dare, and surely you will see what he saw.

Midway through his life, Dante, on the eve of Good Friday, 1300, discovers that he has strayed from the True Way of the religious life, and has wandered into the Dark Wood of Error, where he must spend a miserable night. At sunrise, hopeful once more, he turns to climb the Mount of Joy, only to find that he is distracted and blocked by the Three Beasts of Worldliness: the leopard of malice and fraud, the lion of violence and ambition, and the she-wolf of incontinence.

Terrified, he is driven back down into the Wood, and begins to despair. It is then that the Shade of Virgil comes to his aid, explaining that he represents Human Reason, and has been sent to lead Dante out of Error by another path. He will take Dante as far as reason can, and then will turn him over to another guide, Beatrice, the revelation of Divine Love. Virgil leads and Dante follows.

They begin their descent into the pit, for it is only through the recognition of sin that purification may take place. Arriving at the Gates of Hell, Dante reads an inscription cut deeply into stone:

ABANDON ALL HOPE YE WHO ENTER HERE[4]

Passing through the Gates, they enter an anteroom filled with noise and confusion. Here are the first of the souls in torment whom Dante will meet. Here are the Opportunists, those who, in life, pursued neither good nor evil, "who were neither for God nor Satan, but only for themselves."[5]

Here in Hell, they must pursue for Eternity a banner they cannot catch, neither quite in Hell, nor quite out of it.

These wretches never born and never dead ran naked
    in a swarm of wasps and hornets that goaded them
    the more and the more they fled,
And made their faces stream with bloody gouts of pus
    and tears that dribbled to their feet,
To be swallowed there by loathsome worms and
    maggots.[6]

Because of the darkness of their sin, they run through darkness. As they pursued every passing opportunity in life, so they must now chase an elusive banner forever. Stung by swarms of conscience, feeding the maggots in death, as they produced moral filth in life, they are punished in accordance with their sins. This is the Law of Symbolic Retribution, the Immutable Law of Hell. The punishment is already implied in each sin. Turned back upon the sinner, it causes him to suffer in a way he really has brought upon himself.

This descent into the pit of his own soul is the journey of every pilgrim. No patient in psychotherapy can recover his own beauty and innocence without first facing the ugliness and evil in himself. Jung tells us we have "dealt the devil . . . [no] serious blow by calling him neurosis."[7] The ways in which we live, the experience of our own sinful souls, still is itself our only Hell.

A clear example of the built-in self-torment of neurotic behavior is apparent in the ways of the manipulative patient. Such a man strives for the power to control other people, so that he will not have to experience his own helplessness, and so that he can escape from the fear that others will manipulate him. Trusting in others in the past, as he had to do as a child, resulted in the experience of being used by others, turned this way and that, without regard for his welfare or for how it made him feel. No one seemed to care enough about him for it to be safe to count on them to be considerate, unless he himself could take over and be in control.

Now he is out to make people treat him differently. But he finds, as we all do, that you can't *make* anyone love you. You just have to reveal who you are and take your chances. Oh, sure, you can give a pleasing impression to others, flatter and appease them. Or, you can intimidate other people, threaten and menace them. But whether by cajoling or by coercing, you cannot elicit a gift of love. Instead, you may call forth a reward for good behavior. But then you are stuck with living with the aching feeling in your chest that, if people really knew what you were like, no one would really care about you. Or, if you succeed in getting your own way by bullying other people, then you must live with the dread of retaliation, if ever you should drop your menacing guard.

But perhaps the most poetic, symbolic retribution for being manipulative is that it leaves you completely open to the manipulations of others. He who seems to be taken in by your flattery is merely another manipulator rewarding your offerings as a way of controlling your behavior. And he who gives in to your threats is surely just waiting to get to his feet once more. His surrender is temporary and political, without any quality of loving trust and yielding.

By way of example, Bertolt Brecht somewhere tells the story of a European peasant caught in the holocaust of the Nazi invasion. A Storm Trooper comes to his cottage, drags him out and tells him: "From now on I am in charge. I will live in your house. You will feed me and polish my boots every day. I will be the master and you the servant. If you disagree, I will kill you. Will you submit to me?" Without answering, the peasant gives over his cottage, feeds the invader each day, and polishes his boots. Months later the Allied armies of liberation come through the village. They drag the Storm Trooper out of the cottage. Just as the Allied soldiers are taking the oppressor off to a prison camp, the peasant goes to him, stands proudly before him, and into his face, answers: "No."

The victims of confidence men are always those secret thieves who hope to get something for nothing. That great psychologist, W. C. Fields, used to say: "You can't cheat an honest man." Only the devious manipulator cannot resist the opportunity to believe the illusion that he is in control, that he can get away with it.

I remember early in my practice treating men who "used" prostitutes. All they had to do to control these women was to give them some money and they could manipulate them into doing whatever they wanted. They could make a whore not only do any sexual trick they commanded, but could get her to be nice to them as well. If such men couldn't buy love, at least they could rent it. The women needed the money. The men had it. The women had to give in. The men were contemptuous, superior, in control.

Later in my practice, I began to treat some hookers and strippers. They made it clear to me that the Johns with whom they dealt were suckers. Give them a little sexual excitement, and you could get them to pay all the money they had. Men were so easy to control. I now feel that trying to identify who is controlled, and who is being controlled, is six-five, pick 'em. And when I try sorting out who is the victim and who the perpetrator of manipulation, I can't tell the knife from the wound.

Dante describes Hell as a funnel-shaped cave descending to the center of the Earth. Circular ledges line the inside, Circles of Damnation. Descending into this "kingdom of eternal night,"[8] on each ledge he and Virgil find the damned souls of the perpetrators of increasingly grievous sins, each group tormented for Eternity by ironically fitting punishments. Carnal sinners, who in life betrayed reason by giving in to their every appetite and abandoning themselves to the wild sweep of their passions, are punished in kind, made to live on a dark ledge, swept 'round forever in the whirlwind of Hell's tempest. Gluttons who wallowed in food and drink, producing nothing but garbage, in Hell must wallow in "putrid slush,"[9] while being torn at by Cerebrus, the gluttonous, three-headed hound of the pit. Now it is they themselves who are slavered over.

Hoarders and Wasters are divided into two opposing groups, each of which must roll great Dead Weights of Mundanity at each other until they clash in the middle, each excess punishing the other. In the foul slime of the Marsh of Styx, the Wrathful attack one another. Up through the mud, bubbles rise from the places beneath in which the Sullen are entombed.

Heretics who denied immortality in life, believing instead that with the body dies the soul, must lie forever in open graves surrounded by the flames of God's wrath. In the River of Boiilng Blood lie Murderers and Tyrants, who in life wallowed in the blood of others, doing violence to their neighbors. Panderers and Seducers, who used others for their own purposes, now are driven by whip-carrying, horned demons who force them to hurry along endlessly to serve the foul purposes of their own tormentors. Flatterers pay for having heaped false flattery on others, by living forever in "a river of excrement that seemed the overflow of the world's latrines . . . [forever] smeared with shit."[10]

Hypocrites march in a slow endless procession. Poetically, they are burdened with cloaks of lead, dazzlingly gilded on the outside, and deadweighted on the inside. Falsifiers, who in life deceived the senses of their fellowmen, now in kind have their own senses offended by darkness and filth, by terrible sounds and smells. And those who betrayed people to whom they were bound by special ties are in the final pit of guilt, the pit of souls who denied love, and so denied God. In the dead center of the earth, they must endure the infernal ice frozen by the loss of all human warmth.

And at the very center is Satan, the King of Hell. The beating of his mighty wings sends out the icy Wind of Depravity, the chilling breath of evil. Once having come to the very center of Evil, having faced every sin and seen its consequences, only now can Dante hope to purify his soul. Only by facing life as it is can he find salvation.

Patients in therapy all begin by protesting, "I want to be good." If they cannot accomplish this, it is only because they are "inadequate," can't control themselves, are too anxious, or suffer from unconscious impulses. Being neurotic is being able to act badly without feeling responsible for what you do.

The therapist must try to help the patient to see that he is exactly wrong, that is, that he is lying when he says he wants to be good. He really wants to be bad. Mortality is an empirical issue. Worse yet, he wants to be bad but to have an excuse for his irresponsibility, to be able to say, "But I can't help it."

His only way out is to see that his pilgrimage to the heavenly City must be undertaken along the road through Hell. When we lay claim to the evil in ourselves, we no longer need fear its occurring outside of our control. For example, a patient comes into therapy complaining that he does not get along well with other people; somehow he always says the wrong thing and hurts their feelings. He is really a nice guy, just has this un-

controllable, neurotic problem. What he does *not* want
to know is that his "unconscious hostility" is not his
problem, it's his *solution.* He is really not a nice guy
who wants to be good; he's a bastard who wants to hurt
other people while still thinking of himself as a nice
guy. If the therapist can guide him into the pit of his
own ugly soul, then there may be hope for him. Once
this pilgrim can see how angry and vindictive he is, he
can trace his story and bring it to the light, instead of
being doomed to relive it without awareness. Nothing
about ourselves can be changed until it is first accepted. Jung points out that "the sick man has not to
learn how to get rid of his neurosis but how to bear it.
For the illness is not a superfluous and senseless burden, it is himself; he himself is that 'other' which we
were always trying to shut out."[11]

If we flee from the evil in ourselves, we do it at our
hazard. All evil is potential vitality in need of transformation. To live without the creative potential of our
own destructiveness is to be a cardboard angel.

Much of the time I believe that we are all about as
good and as bad as one another. A greater capacity for
good, such as that to be found in the enlightened
therapist, is matched by his increased capacity for even
greater evil. As for the patient, "at best . . . [he]
should come out of the analysis as he actually is, in
harmony with himself, neither good nor bad, but as a
man truly is, a natural being."[12]

Dante has descended into the Abyss of Evil; he has
had to spend a season in Hell, before he could rise once
more to be illumined by the Divine Light. There is no
sin he could not find within himself. He is as good and
as bad as the rest of us. But even if you should believe
that some men are better than others then I ask you in
the name of myself and all of the others who find that
we have never had a completely *pure* motive in our entire lives: "Even if a man is not good, why should he be
abandoned?"[13]

8. Tale of a Search for Belonging

The anti-hero of Franz Kafka's hauntingly sinister novel, *The Castle*,[1] is a wandering stranger, perhaps a land-surveyor. He is a hapless wayfarer, searching for some confirmation of his identity. He is K., a man with no more name than that. He strives desperately to attain a place for himself within the authority of The Castle, wishing to trade his lonely rootlessness, his permanent homelessness, for a sense of belonging to something greater than himself.

But the harder he tries to make contact with the faceless authorities who run The Castle, the more he is confronted with the frustration of their vagueness and impersonality. He just cannot get the hang of their ambiguous procedures. He is ever in a state of doubt. At times he feels unfairly treated and so responds with ineffectual defiance. But more often, he feels vaguely guilty, as though his frustration must be his own fault. After all, if there is a rule, it must have *some* meaning. There must be some sense to their incomprehensible regulations. In his isolation and impotence, he senses that the problem must be the result of his own basic inferiority.

He is again and again stuck in the obsessional mire of his indecision, his unwillingness to choose between freedom and obligation. He feels that he must keep on trying. There must be a way to satisfy the unclear requirements of the authorities, to behave satisfactorily so that they will accept him. If only he could figure out the rules, then he would follow them.

This wish to satisfy someone greater than the Self, to be found acceptable, to belong at last, is a struggle familiar to many psychotherapy patients. In their lives they waste themselves on wondering how they are doing, on trying to figure out the expectations of others so that they can become *someone* in the eyes of the others. They try to be practical, to be reasonable, to figure it all out in their heads. It is as though if only they could get the words straight in their heads, if only they could find the correct formula, then everything else in their lives would be magically straightened out. They are sure there is a right way to do things, though they have not yet found it. Someone in authority must know. Instead of understanding that ideas are merely feeble intellectual attempts to get a momentary hold on the unceasing flux of life, they act as though Nature imitates Art. It is as though if it were discovered that two and two *really* did not equal four (but five), then at that moment all over the world every machine would stop operating, all of the lights would go out.

Some patients, of course, also approach their therapist with expectations and strategies much like K.'s approach to the Castle authorities. But at best, the psychotherapeutic guru does not play the Castle game. Instead, as O. Hobart Mowrer once pointed out, it is as though the patient and the therapist have sat down to play a game of cards. The hands are dealt out. The patient holds his cards close to his vest, inspecting them carefully. After some deliberation, he selects a card for his first play. He watches the therapist's face carefully for a response to this first attempt at strategy to find out if he has made the right play. Now it is the therapist's turn to play. Much to the patient's amazement, the therapist begins by laying all of his cards on the table, *face up,* ready to encounter the patient transparently, and without guile. It often takes a long while before the patient is willing to do the same.

This disarmingly open mode of being together does not occur in every type of psychotherapy. Merely advertising a journey as a pilgrimage does not guarantee what sort of trip it will be. Szasz has developed socio-economic metaphors for the nature of the psychotherapeutic contract between pilgrim and guru which help us to see what we may expect.[2]

The model that underlies most of what I have to say about this relationship is *Entrepreneurial Psychotherapy*. It occurs most often in a private-practice setting, in which patient and therapist come together as free agents and consenting adults. They are each motivated by self-interest. The relationship is governed by a service contract between seller and buyer, in which expert services are exchanged for money. As political equals, they meet freely, and each is free to terminate the contract at will. The one defines himself as a patient in order to find relief from personal suffering. The other agrees to offer expert services for a fee. The bargain is an equitable one, and the patient's rights to confidentiality and privacy are respected and protected.

At the other end of the contractual spectrum is the model of *Coerced Psythotherapy*. It occurs most often in institutional settings such as prisons and mental hospitals, but is not unknown in the bureaucracy of clinics, or even at times in private practice. In this situation, the patient does not freely choose to seek out the therapist's services. He comes instead under the duress of threatened sanctions by the court, or under the pressure of the family or community whom he has made anxious, or because "therapy" may be his only hope of regaining his political and social freedom. The social power of the therapist is inherent in his role. The inequality of the participants comes closer to that of warden and prisoner than to one man being paid to help another. The real client seeking relief is the family or the community who sees to it that the patient is vulnerable to the expert, and who pays the latter's fees. The goal is not the relief of the patient's suffering, but rather the re-establishment of social control. Consequently, as the community's agent (rather than his own or the patient's), the therapist does not value or protect his patient's privacy and confidentiality.

The third alternative is a model that may be called *Bureaucratic Psychotherapy*. It stands somewhere be-

tween the first two. While it offers some of the advantages
of the first model (that of free agents), it is more insidious than the coercive model because the face of the
enemy is not clear. The therapist works for a non-
residential agency such as a clinic or a school, and the
patient may or may not be a freely participating adult.
The therapist is a double-agent whose contract and
loyalties belong as much to his commitment to his
agency and to the community as to the patient. The
best and worst of social welfare attitudes are at play as
the therapist decides on the goals (for the patient's own
good), so that the patient may stay out of trouble and
accomplish some "worthwhile" social objectives. While
the bureaucratic psychotherapist is not a jailer (like the
coercive therapist), the social conditions under which
the often underprivileged patient is offered the favor of
welfare-therapy clearly imply the superiority of the expert. In this ambiguous setting, the confidentiality and
privacy of the patient are not seen (by the agency
staff) as crucial to his well-being. Consequently, protection of the patient's rights is often incomplete and
capricious.

The patient's relationship to the clinical bureaucracy
is as frustratingly vague as K.'s place vis-à-vis The
Castle.

This sinister ambiguity has too often also been evident in the patient's early life. Bob grew up in a family
world in which it was clear that there were rules, but
just what those rules were he could never figure out.
From time to time, his mother would get wildly upset,
fling abuse at Bob, and punish him cruelly, but he
could never quite figure out just what he had done
wrong. The reason for this was that the stated family
regulations seemed to keep changing. As a child, he
never did discover that law and (dis)order in his family
all turned on an unstated meta-rule. That unspoken
principle was that whatever happened to make mother
anxious at any given moment was absolutely forbidden.
The kinds of behavior that bugged his mother changed
erratically, always without warning or explanation. By

the time I met Bob, he had become a psychotherapist, partly in an attempt to discover the rules that governed other people's behavior.

Bob's father was largely unknown to him, except as an important man whose time was taken up by a demanding career. He was a public figure, and Bob was to take on faith that the old man's time and activities were dedicated to fulfilling some greater extra-familial expectations, demands that Bob was somehow always too young to be able to understand (so no one ever took the trouble to try to explain them to him). His father "discovered" that he had a son, when there was fortuitous coincidence that brought them together.

There were "reasons" at that time that his father had to retire, "a matter of principle." Bob was fourteen, and was trying out the one piece of guidance his paternal model had provided. He had learned to hustle. At this time, when his father suddenly began to spend some time at home, the son had worked up a monopoly on lawn mowing in the neighborhood. Father took an immediate interest, demonstrated by taking Bob out to buy an expensive power mower. By the time I met Bob, he was still working his ass off, toiling too-long hours and volunteering to take on all of the most "challenging" (translate: "difficult") tasks available to the staff of the clinic at which he worked.

He was a talented young man, who worked and worked and worked, but was never sure he had done enough, and secretly resented his obligations. His guilt about not doing enough was what most of us feel when we are secretly angry that so much seems expected of us. He vacillated between believing that he was doing his job perfectly, that he had nothing to learn, and that he did not know what the hell he was up to. It never occurred to him to try to figure out what he himself wanted to do, to ask for help, advice, or explanations. Needless to say, he married a young woman whose shtick was "naïveté," who was overly impressed with her husband's worldliness. He had to school her as to what life was all about. Unfortunately, before entering treatment, she often found herself getting terribly upset about some of the ways in which he acted, but could never explain to him just what was wrong.

One day during a couples-group psychotherapy session, Bob unhooked from his struggle with his wife to complain about his "depression" about not feeling competent at work. He had taken on a job no one else wanted, running a psychotherapy group for criminal offenders who only came to the clinic because they were under threat of being returned to prison. It was the sort of impossibly unrewarding job that I had long ago given up trying because it did not seem that doing it would be good for me. My own basic first principle had finally become: take care of yourself!

The evening before, he had waited at the clinic, and not a single group member had shown up. He dreaded going back, and did not know what to do. He had no clear rules of his own as to how to handle this situation and did not know what kind of claims he had the right to make on the people he was treating. He was sure that I couldn't help, that he would just have to suffer through, figuring out what he "ought to" do. I pointed out his refusal to ask for clarification, and assured him that I certainly could help him, that I had been there myself, remembered how awful it felt, and knew that some things were just too hard to do alone. When he questioned my understanding of the situation, I told him that the rule that his family had neglected to teach him was that it is important for each of us to be in touch with his own feelings, to know his own wishes. His wish, he said, was to be able to give up the too tough job of leader of that uncooperative group of offenders. I thought that that must be right for him to do, simply because it was what he himself wanted to do. When was he going to do it? I asked. He explained and explained that it was not possible, that he was merely a pawn, caught in the meshing machinery of clinic policy and Department of Correction demands. The group encouraged him to act on his wishes, to define his own situation, to take his chances. I laughed and laughed at him for not doing so, assuring him that fools like him made it so much easier for me to get away with doing just whatever suited me best. Over the years it had become clearer to me that the more of a claim I made on the world, the more often I got what I wanted.

He left that session seemingly unconvinced. There were rules out there. They were always made by someone else, and it was up to helpless little guys like him to try to figure them out so that they could avoid punishment. But over the months he had accomplished enough in his own therapeutic pilgrimage to bring his efforts to fruition. He returned the following week, transformed and astonished. It turned out that he had accepted my permission to do what he really wanted to do. All I had really done for him was to give him permission to do without parental permission. Their rules were too obscure, and no longer really relevant, so he could make his own rules, if he dared.

The morning after the last session, he had instructed the clinic secretary to send out a letter to each group member telling him that he was discontinuing the group because of their expressed lack of interest. He also sent out a duplicate memo to that effect to the head of the Department of Correction and to his own clinic director. Then he put himself through an anxiety attack while awaiting the Olympian lightning bolt, the *nemesis* with which the gods punish any puny mortal who displays the *hubris* to challenge them. Still he felt strangely relieved even before the consequences of his acts were to become clear. I assured him, before learning the outcome, that whatever the results, he had done just right, he had honored his own wishes.

The results turned out to be spectacular, but that was just gravy as far as I was concerned. The members of the offenders' group didn't protest. They really hadn't wanted to join the group in the first place. The clinic director acquiesced, made it clear that he had long trusted Bob's judgment and his willingness to act on his own wishes. The Department of Correction went on to offer to hire him as a consultant who would guide their policy decisions (at a substantially higher salary). Once he was willing to own his wishes and to act on them, he went from being a pawn to being a pivot. Ironically, he has not taken the offer, deciding instead to try private practice, where he can make the rules and be his own boss.

There is a tyranny inherent in the reciprocities of every system. Rules for a group always violate individual rights. Both slave and master are trapped and dehumanized (though the bulk of my sympathy goes readily to the more explicitly oppressed of the pair). It is, of course, necessary to have rules and procedures if we wish to accomplish large and complex tasks, but the question of whether or not it is worth the cost must be perennially re-examined. Anarchy could never get a man to the moon, but it may become the only mode that can allow us to survive on the earth.

Catholic theologians make a distinction between the visible church and the invisible church. The invisible church is the ideal expression of what Christ had in mind. The visible church is the imperfect concretization of it in a social-political organization run by mortal men. All institutions fall short of their purposes. Sometimes it seems to me that they are more trouble than they are worth, that they bring with them evils at least equivalent to the social good that they provide. The family is the social institution that I trust most, and there certainly have been times when even that has seemed like a mistake to me.

As a therapist, I do not consider myself a "Shrink." I wish to help expand consciousness, not to diminish it. I am not interested in getting people to "adjust" to our rather unsatisfactory culture. At the same time, I am not a "Radical Therapist" preaching revolution and social change. Instead, I hope to help the pilgrims who seek my guidance to see that all rules are mere conventions, games that one can play or not. It is only necessary to recognize that they are games, to do what you wish, and to face the consequences of your behavior.

It is necessary first to teach some patients how to play, before they can become free to know and follow their own wishes. A revolution must be started in their heads. They are trapped more by the rules in their own minds than by social expectations and constraints. A patient named Bernard provides a relevant case in point.

Though Bernard had accomplished a great deal, he somehow never felt satisfied. He was a bright young graduate student, so well thought of in his field that he was already being allowed to take on projects that usually fell to more experienced professionals. His wife was a lovely young woman who loved and admired him so much that she never made any important decisions without turning to him for counsel. He handled so many things so well that it was often easier for him to work things out himself than to ask anyone for help. That made it difficult for him to choose to enter psychotherapy. He came to see me only because he felt that he had a responsibility to get everything figured out.

He was bewildered by my setting up our relationship as one in which I already knew all about the kind of problems he had, and therefore had no need to listen to any of his explanations. His job in therapy, I suggested, was to learn how to play, though even that was not required, because it didn't really matter what he did, or why.

During one particular session, he was struggling with trying to figure out why his father had expected so much from him and given him so little. I laughed at his attempts to figure out what was wrong with him that his father should have treated him that way, or alternately when he speculated about father's "unconscious motivation" (or what the old man had *really* been up to). I told him that it didn't matter, and that figuring all this out was just a way of still trying to please a father who had never tried to please him. Bernard said that that wasn't the point. It was just the way he was. He had to get a thing figured out, or he would just worry and worry over it without being able to turn his attention to anything else.

I told him that I knew just how to help him with this, but it would require that for the next five minutes he do whatever I asked of him, no matter how silly it might seem. Just five minutes, and then I promised I would let him go back to worrying and figuring, if he still wanted to. We had been enough good places together already so that he agreed to trust me on this. Besides, he was sure that he would still want to return to his obsessing.

He was perplexed when I asked him to tell me all that he knew about the duck-billed platypus. He tried, describing it as "a strange looking bird, no, an animal with a bird-bill, from Australia and New Zealand, all extinct now." I told him how delighted I was that he knew so much about my favorite creature. He protested that he did not know enough about it to do what I asked next, that is, to make up a story about a duck-billed platypus. I assured him that the only problem was that he might already have too much information to go on, but that there was really no way in which his story could come out wrong anyway.

Reluctantly he began, only warming to his story after he got rolling. "I'll make up a story that begins with an oddly shaped egg, at the edge of a stream. There are no other creatures around, but the eggshell is beginning to crack. Whatever is inside is hatching itself. From out of the shell emerges a most peculiar-looking little guy, almost looks like an otter with a duck's bill. He stumbles around trying to walk but he doesn't know how to get his feet to work right. He flaps his flippers but he can't work out any way to fly, either. Then he discovers his reflection in the stream, and nothing seems to go with any other part. He looks like a stuck-together collection of bits and pieces who can't figure out what he is supposed to be. He sits on the bank, dejected, not able to figure it all out." "And then what?" I asked. "That's it, just sits and worries." "That's not a story. It has no ending," I insisted. We struggled silently. Finally, he gave in. "Okay, the little guy gets up and looks at the stream, not at his reflection, but at the water. It seems cool and splashy. He still doesn't know how he got to be all stuck together like this, but fuck it!" Chuckling with delight, he goes on: "The little guy just jumps into the water and plays and plays and plays and plays. He can do that without even having to figure it out."

Afterwards Bernard used the rest of the session to "just sit around and feel good." He didn't know just how I had gotten him to feel so happy and relaxed but he found that later he could do it for himself, without ever quite being able to figure out just how it worked.

So often intent on learning the rules of the game of life, the patient/pilgrim often tries hard to get the guru/therapist to instruct him. He is sure that there must be more to life than he has been able to establish, some hidden order to be discovered that will provide the key to happiness, to perfection, to a problem-free life. The therapist seems to know what *he* is doing. Surely *he* has discovered and mastered the rules of the game. The patient cannot believe that the therapist has only learned to play "the game of no game."[3]

What is he to make of the realization that the only rules that the therapist follows and teaches are *meta-rules*, rules about rules. The therapist thereby teaches that all rules are merely arbitrary conventions, sometimes useful but never necessary, sometimes timely but never of enduring relevance. The therapist uses rules tentatively as guidelines, but never takes them more seriously than he takes himself. They are no more than mock standards from which to deviate. He has no rule that he is not willing to break. He may move with seeming consistency, but only when it is viewed in the light of his detours, contradictions, and turnabouts. He no longer believes in the existence of the Law, and is no longer willing to put responsibility elsewhere. He will run his own life as best he can, and take the consequences without making excuses. And even this freedom is not his as a permanent achievement. At each moment it threatens to slip away and must be reclaimed. If he is to live his own life, then again and again, for the remainder of that life, he must trade the illusion of certainty for the holy insecurity of never knowing for sure what it's all about.

It is no wonder that therapists are often fascinated by Zen koans, shamanistic trances, and other games. All these serve as reminders of the arbitrariness of the rules that bring the temporary appearance of order to this absurdly chaotic, madly entropic life we live. *Eleusis* and *Ultima*[4] are the only table games that I have ever seen played at the annual workshops of the American Academy of Psychotherapists.

The first, *Eleusis,* is an unusual sort of card game. It differs from ordinary card games, which each have a set of rules known to every player in advance. When you start to play a hand of *Eleusis,* you do not know the key rule that will govern the play of that hand. It is only by figuring out this secret rule that you will be able to make the right plays and have a chance to win. But each new hand calls for a new dealer, who in turn gets to make up a new key rule. In order to have any chance of winning, a player must recognize the complete arbitrariness of the hidden rule. He must be flexible enough to try out one thing after another, and to abandon those strategies that turn out not to work. The dealer does not explain the rule during the play. He only tells whether a particular play is "right" or "wrong," and each player must be guided by his own experiences.

Ultima is a complex variation on chess, played with conventional pieces and chessboard, but in rather unconventional ways. Its rules of play mimic the subtle, hidden ways by which people sometimes try to control and dominate one another. In most other war games, there is only one straightforward method of capture (such as the short leap in checkers, or the interception of the captured piece by moving into its space in chess).

In *Ultima,* the methods of capture are more varied and subtler. Even the distance a piece may move depends on how deeply into enemy territory it has penetrated. By way of example:

1. The *Withdrawer* can capture the piece next to it, by moving *away* from the piece.

2. The *Coordinator* captures by trapping the enemy piece *between* itself and another ally.

3. The deadly *Immobilizer* does *not* capture and remove a piece from the board. Instead it *paralyzes* any piece it stands beside. Its power is restored if the Immobilizer moves away. The immobilized piece can only escape by making the *Suicide Move,* by removing itself so as to clear the way for an attack on the Immobilizer.

4. The *Chameleon* can use any form of capture, so long as it does to pieces what they do to other pieces. The manner of attack *changes* according to which piece it is attempting to capture. Of course, no Chameleon can capture another Chameleon.

These *Ultima* methods of capture all serve as apt metaphors for the games people play. At the same time, all of the best of the games that therapists play help to keep them aware of the contingency basis on which all rules are founded. Immutable laws derived from an infallible source are a comfort, but only in the same way that being kept a prisoner can bring with it a sense of security.

It is not necessary to discard all laws. Yet one of the results of the patient's pilgrimage may be a new outlook on moral laws. As he gains a deeper sense of his own identity, a sense of self based on knowing his own wishes and trusting his feelings, he may develop a framework of *situational ethics.* Rules will come to serve as tentative guidelines. Each act will have to be judged as a personal experience, in terms of its existential meaning, rather than by checking it out against a rule carved on a stone tablet long ago and far away.

Even the Mosaic Law, the Ten Commandments that

serve as the ground of the Judeo-Christian tradition, comes alive when its foundations are shaken in this way. We can come to see that the proscriptions against coveting, stealing, and even murdering are no more than reminders that men everywhere will always be tempted to these excesses. So it is that God tugs at a pilgrim's sleeve telling him to remember that he is only human. He must be his own man, remain in exile, and belong to himself. He must pay attention to his own feelings and to the meaning of what he does, if he is to be for himself, and yet for others as well.

9. Tale of a Holy Warrior

John Bunyan chose to spend almost twelve years in prison, chose an anti-Establishment, religious non-conformity that cost him his freedom, while it earned him the opportunity to witness for what he believed in. He was a seventeenth-century English workingman, the son of a tinker, who became a dissenting preacher in the service of Puritanism, that "austere disciplining of life in the service of a fervid religious faith."[1]

He wrote to tell his tale, to find his way, and to encourage his shepherdless congregation to face up to both political oppression and human temptation. He asks them to remember as they read his tale: "I have sent you here enclosed a drop of that honey that I have taken out of the carcass of a lion (Judg. 14:5-9). I have eaten thereof myself also, and am much refreshed thereby."[2]

The most memorable rendering of his spiritual struggle is his allegorical novel, *The Pilgrim's Progress*.[3] The personal urgency of his journey is clear from the very beginning:

As I walked through the wilderness of this world, I lighted on a certain place, where was a den; and I laid me down in that place to sleep; and as I slept I dreamed a dream. I dreamed, and behold I saw a man clothed with rags, standing in a certain place, with his face from his own house, a book in his hand, and a great burden upon his back. I looked, and saw him open the book and read therein; and as he read, he wept and trembled: and not being able longer to

contain, he broke out with a lamentable cry, saying:
"What shall I do?"[4]

Many patients about to enter onto the pilgrimage of
psychotherapy also find themselves turned toward this
venture by disturbing dreams, night visions that are
prophetic statements of their spiritual/emotional crises.
I remember one tortured young clergyman whose underlying motivation for seeking help was the growing
recognition that he had learned the tricks of successful
ministry in the absence of really feelingful spiritual substance. The superficial manipulative skills, which had
served to make him appealing to many, were growing
ineffective as he began to realize that his brand of in-
spirational goodness was a subtle form of evil, that he
was up to no good. The week of his first meeting with
me, he had dreamed that he was a powerful warlock
casting spells. But in this dream he found all at once
that his magical gestures and incantations no longer
forked any lightning. He hexed impotently with his
hands and muttered sorcerer's gibberish, only to discover that for the first time no one was controlled by
his witchcraft. That was the beginning of a long struggle
which gradually allowed him to reclaim and renew his
faith, not through control of others but through surrender to himself.

Bunyan's dream-figure is Christian, the spiritual pilgrim of this allegory. The book is the Holy Bible,
through which he has become aware of the prophecy
of his coming destruction. He and his entire community
are all to be "burned with fire from heaven."[5] On his
back is the weight of the burden of his own sin. What is
he to do?

He tries in vain to rouse the others, but finds that
each person can only save his own soul. A man called
Evangelist appears and counsels him to *Fly from the
wrath to come.*[6] He must follow the shining light to the
Wicket Gate. There, if he knocks, he will be answered
and told what he must do.

So begins Christian's pilgrimage. It is beset with hazardous temptations, but there are unexpected helpers along the way. Early on his journey, Christian falls into the Slough of Despond, a bog that cannot be cleared up because it is "descent whither the scum and filth that attends conviction for sin . . . runs continually."[7] This conviction of sin is the awakening of the soul, the first stage in the Puritan experience of conversion. As in psychotherapy, confronting one's own personal garbage is the way to begin.

Further on along the way, Christian encounters Mr. Wordly-Wiseman from the city of Carnal-Policy. He advises Christian to give up this "dangerous and troublesome" journey, fraught as it is with "wearisomeness, painfulness, hunger, perils, nakedness, sword, lions, dragons, darkness, and in a word, death, and what not."[8] Christian is tempted to give up striving "to enter at the strait gate."[9] but he discovers that there is no salvation through moral righteousness. The failure of this attempt is the second stage in the Puritan psychology of conversion. Easy cop-out solutions are of no more help to the Christian wayfarer than they are to the psychotherapy patient.

At the Gate, with the help of Patience, Christian learns that he can only be illuminated through the gradual education of Bible study and meditation. This third stage of his conversion is the equivalent of the patient's learning that psychotherapeutic change also comes in bits and pieces, which must be paid for with time and painful efforts.

Further up the straight road, Christian finds his way fenced on either side by the Wall of Salvation. With great difficulty he runs to a place where the Cross stands, and there his burden of sin falls from his back into an open sepulcher. Here then is Redemption, the final stage of his conversion. Yet it is not "the end of the drama, but the beginning."[10] When a psychotherapy patient gives up just trying to feel better in recognition that he must instead be willing to change, that too is a new beginning.

The idea that every pilgrimage itself, and not its end point, is the spiritual goal has always been difficult to grasp. Christ came, and with the revolutionary zeal of a true shaman, he turned Judaism upside down. He was opposed by the priestly class of Pharisees who had divided their countrymen into two classes of saints and sinners. The Pharisees themselves were, of course, to be numbered among the righteous, while the others (the Sadducees) were condemned as transgressors. They sought to maintain the religious establishment. He came to renew the Law by overturning it with revolutionary reinterpretation. Christ roused the multitudes, and set them off once more upon the journey of salvation.

For a while, there was an atmosphere of true religious fellowship, of loving and searching. But, as ever, too soon the charisma of Christ's inspired leadership became routinized. The practical considerations about how to maintain the Church and expand its power drained the spiritual fire and excitement of being an early Christian. Instead one had to learn to be a *good* Christian. No longer was it important to live out one's salvation. Instead, the point became to achieve it and keep it.

Salvation, the attainment of the Kingdom of God, became something to work toward, a pagan utopian ideal, a perfect place to go to, a pilgrimage with an end goal. Some of this quality of achievement of ends is apparent in *The Pilgrim's Progress,* but at his best, Christian, Bunyan's "man on the march," is more committed to the going than to the getting there. Latter-day Christian Existentialists have illuminated this distinction, by pointing out that being "good" in order to achieve the future rewards of Heaven is a pietistic striving characterized more by pride than by virtue. The kingdom is come. It is here, now, at each given moment for each of us. It need only be accepted to be achieved. Each moment of Salvation must be encountered for itself as part of the spiritual journey. But we do not get to keep it forever. We do not get to stay in the Kingdom of God, except as we spend our lives on the road. Eternity does not mean "forever." Eternity means beyond time. If we live as pilgrims, then at each moment of revelation, we step out of History and into Nature. The Kingdom is come for those who would grasp it, but at each moment, it must be regrasped, and then at the next moment regrasped once more. The openness to salvation must be reasserted again and again and again. The only way to be saved is to spend your lifetime on a pilgrimage.

Like Bunyan's pilgrim, the psychotherapy patient becomes a lonely wayfarer, a back-packing, foot-sore, simple, honest man. For such a Holy Warrior, "the man who fully exists is a man on the march."[11] It is the journey itself that is his salvation.

It does not matter (for the psychotherapy experience) what the journey is *about*. It matters only that the patient stay on the road. The "aboutness" is the same pseudo-problem of "content" that was created in the world of Art when "people used to ask what a painting was *about*."[12]

> In individual therapy we may get the patient to focus on his past history. In group therapy, we may encourage the patient's curiosity about the group process. Some of what occurs as the patient reluctantly takes on these tasks is that he can begin to lose himself in the sense of giving himself over to the assigned work. As this unhooks him from his willful, self-sorry demand for someone to give him relief right now, a new possibility arises: The patient can now begin to experience the therapist and the other patients as real people with selves of their own; as people who have meaning outside of himself, who can therefore be meaningful to him, and who can ultimately put him in touch with the meaning of his own life.[13]

Marshall McLuhan's conceptions are helpful in understanding the importance of form over content in psychotherapy and in other spiritual pilgrimages. In discussing the impact of the evolving technology of communication media (from primitive tribal storytelling by the elders, through the advent of the printed word, to our current electronic maelstrom), McLuhan teaches us that *the medium* is the message."[14] That is to say, the personal and social consequences of any medium result more from the shape and the scale of the message than from its content.

He also distinguishes between "hot" and "cool" media. A hot medium like television has "high definition," in the sense that it is so well-filled with data that the viewer needs bring little to his participation besides passive reception. A cool medium, such as a book, on the other hand, has low definition in that it provides less information, leaving much of the experience to be filled in by the reader. "Cool media are high in participation or completion by the audience."[15] Psychotherapy is a fine example of such a cool medium.

When applied to psychotherapy, the thesis that "the medium is the message" means that the meta-assumptions and the parameters of psychotherapy, in themselves, constitute the "cure," regardless of the content of what the patient discusses. The very act of focusing attention on himself (by telling his tale) already changes things. Behavior of which he is aware is already different from that same behavior unobserved by the patient. In fact, the mere act of entering the pilgrimage of the psychotherapeutic journey is itself a transformingly courageous acknowledgment of the existence of critical problems and a daring expression of the longing for resolution.

Immersion in the medium of psychotherapy, starting down that difficult road, is already an interruption of some aspects of the problem-engendering behavior and attitudes.

The guru facilitates this interruption merely by defining himself as "the Therapist." As the Therapist, he is freed from following any social rules of politeness or appeasement. He need not honor appearances, answer questions, or even be "reasonable." Consequently, no matter what the content of the dialogue, the patient is faced with the breakdown of the social-expectation games and intellectual headtripping by which he can ordinarily keep from changing or becoming aware of himself and other people.

Once in therapy, he finds himself in a new context, one that demands that he pay attention to his feelings and that he discover that in his dealings with other people things are often not what they appear to be. As a pilgrim, he is committed to enduring hardships as an act of faith. He meets on a regular and continuing basis with another human being who again will turn his focus back onto himself and the relationship of the community of men that exists between them. He will have to deal with his responsibility for what he does, at the same time that he discovers that he is not fully in control of all of his life.

And like Bunyan's pilgrim, the psychotherapy patient will have to learn to fend for himself, to become a lonely wayfarer whose whole life becomes one long, transforming pilgrimage. Being in treatment may show him the way he is to journey, but it will be up to him to reclaim his salvation continually by remaining on the march for the rest of his life.

10. Tale of the Eternal Jew

The *Legend of the Wandering Jew*[1] has its roots in myths and sagas that predate the Bible. It reflects man's unrelenting concern with guilt and redemption, his search for meaning, his fascination with the origin of life and the mystery of death. These profound and ultimately insoluble preoccupations are timeless and universal. They are the stuff of which folk tales are made.

The anti-hero of the legend appears in the folklore of many cultures in varied guises. Only the theme remains the same: *the problem of redemption.* I shall call this wanderer by his medieval name, *Ahasuerus.* When Christ struggled up the hill of Golgotha, it was Ahasuerus who would not let him rest, but would only mock the suffering Jesus, saying: "Why do you loiter? Go faster, Jesus, go faster!" And it was to Ahasuerus that Jesus turned saying: "I am going, but you shall wait until I return."

And so it was that Ahasuerus was condemned to roam the earth in despair, awaiting Christ's return, "so cursed *it had been good for that man if he had not been born.*"[2] This homeless wanderer through Eternity goes from place to place. When asked when he arrived, he inevitably answers, "Yesterday." When asked when he will leave, he always replies, "Tomorrow." This Eternal Jew is a metaphor for all of the Children of Israel, and the Jews are everyman's symbol of exiled humanity. It is said that the definition of a Jew is that he is just like everyone else, *only more so.*

The unredeemed wanderer figures in Asiatic folklore and appears in the tales of primitive cultures, as well. Even within the Judeo-Christian traditions, the Eternal

Jew has many faces. At times he has been identified as
the anti-Christ who stands over against Jesus. Yet it is
only in terms of his vivid expression of man's finitude
and fallibility that Divine Love can be defined. Without
the betrayal of Judas Iscariot, there would have been no
Crucifixion, and no Resurrection. That Judas is Everyman is implied in Christ's admonition to those who
would follow him to bear the Cross:

> Verily I say unto you, There be some standing here,
> which shall not taste of death, till they see the Son of
> Man coming in his kingdom.[3]

Adam's son, Cain, is the first eternal wanderer to appear in the Bible. Denounced by God for killing his
own brother, Cain is condemned to be a fugitive and a
vagabond upon the earth. And lest anyone finding him
should kill him, the mark of God is put upon him.

The Jewish version of the wanderer is sadly sweet-
ened in the story of Elijah. God chooses Elijah to remind mankind of the Coming of the Messiah. He will
not taste of death till then, but he is no pariah. He
roams the world to teach men to be good, and his ar-
rival is always joyously welcomed.

The repentant sinner is ever God's favorite child.
Every man lives in a state of vague Kafkaesque guilt.
Like Job, we all feel that if we suffer, there must be a
reason; that if we are unhappy, it must be that we deserve it. So it is that we long for forgiveness, for redemption. After all, if we admitted that we lived in a
random universe, where virtue is often not rewarded
and evil not punished, there would never be any hope
of our being forgiven for our sins and taken care of
forever by a lovingly all-powerful God.

It is the very nature of man's living in the world that
he must contend with certain existential anxieties that
are built into his situation.[4] He judges himself, but
hears the accusations and the verdict as the voice of
God, the Fates, or Society. He tries to be good, but
knows that his behavior is permeated with evil inten-

tions as well. He feels free and responsible for his life, and yet knows that in so many ways he does not control his own destiny. When all else fails, at the very least he can take himself and his life seriously. But how often in the quiet of the darkness does each of us ask himself: "What the hell does it all mean? What's it all about?"

Wayfarers on the pilgrimage of psychotherapy often long for a sort of psychological redemption, for a time when all their troubles will be over. Their guru image of me is the fantasy that I represent secular salvation in the form of complete Maturity. To this image they impute characteristics that not only do I not possess, but to which I do not even aspire. Often for a time I am seen by the patient as being beyond anxiety, without conflicts, free of weaknesses, never foolish, incapable of evil, and always happy.

I experience this idolization as a terrible burden, rather than as the gift of admiration that its wrappings imply. Because I am strong and he is weak, because I am wise and he is foolish, because I am so important to him while he means so little to me, the patient insists that I must take care of him. In our interactions I must be sure not to hurt him, but he can treat me any way he damn pleases. Because I know that we are both unredeemed sinners, both wandering in exile, each equally vulnerable, I will not accept his burdensome illusion that we are not the same.

Part of the reason that patients insist that I have already attained salvation is that if it were otherwise, how could I save them? Certainly at the beginning of treatment, they do not imagine for a moment that each of us must save himself. *How* this experienced inequity between pilgrim and guru comes about is as important as *why* it occurs. I get to seem so strong and wise as a function of the patient's disowning the responsibility of his own strength and wisdom by projecting these assets onto my not-so-wide shoulders.

Of course, in moments of desperately felt need to get beyond the ambiguity of my own strong/weak, wise/foolish personality, I am tempted to make the trade. He can have my inadequacies in exchange for the personal powers he gives over to me. I often warn patients that my opium dreams of omniscience, omnipotence, and unbearable pleasures endlessly experienced will certainly tempt me to go along with his making me into Mr. Wonderful. I do not simply abandon myself to indulging in these pleasant fantasies. They always turn out so badly. But I can so easily be fooled that it behooves the patient to pay attention to that possibility.

After all, he has been a neurotic longer than I have been a therapist. He has been fooling people by getting them to accept him as being too helpless to take care of of himself, fooling them longer than I have been struggling not to get fooled. Surely he will be able to fool me from time to time. But when he does, if he wins, he loses. For then I will be of no help to him at all. His only salvation lies in his willingness to become curious about these pitfalls, to become aware of the times that I may try to take advantage of him by pretending that he is as little as he fears he is and that I am as great as he hopes I am. If he is willing to tug at my sleeve, to point out to me how he is taking me in, to help me not to yield to my arrogance, then perhaps together we will be able to avoid getting permanently stuck. If he can forgive me for my weaknesses, then perhaps he can begin to accept his own strengths.

Patients are often disappointed to learn that I too wander unredeemed, that I am no better off than they are. Eventually, they may realize comfort implied in my turning out to be just another struggling human being. At least then I can bring a fellow-pilgrim sort of understanding to his journey. Recognition of my all-too-obvious fallibility can provide the relief of learning that some happiness is possible without his having to reach some state of perfection. But before my own vulnerability and finitude can be a source of solace, its exposure is experienced by the patient as an irritating disappointment.

He was sure that if he worked hard enough, suffered

long enough, or (failing that) at least if he were to be rescued by me, then Nirvana could be his. He can bear his pain for a while if only someday, someway, he will be able to reach a state of blissful perfection, a time when he will have no more conflicts, anxieties, or uncertainties. As I come toppling down off the pedestal on which he has placed me, he is horrified to learn that enlightenment does not provide perfection. Instead, it simply offers the pedestrian possibility of living with the acceptance of imperfection.

I remember a group therapy session when one of the patients was reluctantly turning this corner. He would accept it, he said, but he wouldn't like the idea of having to solve problems every day for the rest of his life. My co-therapist told him that it was not required that he like it. She shared her own displeasure, saying: "I remember that when I first discovered what life was really like, I was furious. I guess I'm still kind of mad sometimes."

What then is a man to do when he realizes that his exiled wandering is to be a lifelong pilgrim, a journey that ends in oblivion rather than in Paradise? Camus crystalized life's absurdity when he wrote: "There is but one truly serious philosophical problem, and that is suicide."[5] There is only *this* life. Live it, or give it up! It does no good to choose to live it reluctantly hedging by whining that it's not sufficient, that someone must make it better for you.

Many pilgrims feel that they can accept their sufferings in this ambiguous, imperfect, mixed bag of a life, if only some guru can tell them why it should be this way. If there is some reason for their suffering, some explanation for their unhappiness, some purpose to their enduring the ups and downs of living, then it's a deal. Otherwise, they will hold out, stubbornly digging in their heels. They do not see that this only results in doubling their grief by making them unhappy about being unhappy.

Like Job, they lament their lot, protesting that they do not deserve to be treated so badly. They demand

justice, or at least a bit of mercy. They experience their
trials as abandonment by God (or some other neglect-
ful parent), without realizing that it is by fussing that
they abandon their own tie to humanity. The experienced alienation of the neurotic is the self-sorry separation from the community of other lonely wanderers.

Like Job, they wail complainingly:

Why is light given to him that is in misery,
    and life to the bitter in soul,
who long for death, but it comes not,
    and dig for it more than for hid treasures;
who rejoice exceedingly,
    and are glad, when they find the grave?
Why is light given to a man whose way is hid,
    whom God has hedged in?
For my sighings come as my bread,
    and my groanings are poured out like water.
For the thing that I fear comes upon me,
    and what I dread befalls me.
I am not at ease, nor am I quiet;
    I have no rest; but trouble comes.[6]

Though Job started out as an innocent, a good man
upon whom life's misfortunes randomly descended, he
ended up being a pest. If God had no reason up front
to plague him with these pains and losses, He might well
have been bugged with Job after listening to his willful
insistence that he could not possibly stand living his
only life.

When a psychotherapy patient does do the work of
facing up to some of what he must endure, he is often
rewarded by a sense of increased freedom and joy.
However, as he comes to realize that there will be no
light without some darkness, no rest without further
toil, he may balk disappointedly to find that troubles
never end. New solutions lead to new problems. New
freedom leads to new responsibilities.

I remember one young man whose father had demanded a great deal from him without ever helping him

to accomplish what was expected. All through his early years, his father simply handed him his message to Garcia. He was assigned difficult tasks for which he often was unready. Without guidance or support, he was expected to deliver results. As he grew up he came to feel harried and inadequate, driven to take on any obstacle that might come up, but never feeling confident enough to enjoy his accomplishments.

During the course of psychotherapy, he began to take the pressure off himself. He learned that it was all right to ask for help. One of the many satisfying outcomes of his growth was that he learned to carry out his work assignments one step at a time, delegating responsibility where needed, seeking guidance from his superiors. He came to understand that his father had asked too much of him and given him too little. He had to face his disappointment at having had so unloving a father in order to be easier on himself and to recognize his own worth.

His increased ease, freedom, and efficiency at work led to his being given the opportunity to take on new administrative responsibilities. He approached his new assignments with confidence and excitement, only to find that the unfamiliar tasks awakened his old panicky drive to somehow get them done entirely on his own, quickly and without error. He messed some things up, and came to his next therapy session berating himself for being a fuck-up.

I mocked him, saying that I couldn't understand why he didn't do everything right the first time, no matter how new or difficult his job might be. His pouting gave way to a brief angry outburst at *my* expecting too much of him. We both laughed, and it was good to be back together again. I kidded him about never being able to reach that place beyond error at which I had arrived. He began to ask me more seriously about what it was like for me, now that I had outgrown my naïveté. I told him with pleasure of how I had learned to overcome my early difficulties as a therapist.

The example that I chose to discuss was how difficult

it had been for me to deal realistically with issues of
salary and fees as a therapist because of old childhood
confusion about the emotional meaning of financial
expectations. And then with considerably less pleasure,
I told him how recently I had goofed anew. My old
financial inexpertness was again at play as I awkwardly
approached a publisher with my writing. Like the
patient, as of old, I had not sought sufficient guidance,
feeling that after all I should be able to handle this
new situation on my own. As a result, I again paid for
my insistence that I had to solve my problem once and
for all. I asked for and received too small an advance
on royalties without realizing that this meant less commitment by the publisher to promote my book.

The patient understood. In that exchange, we each
learned again a bit more clearly that our old problems
would remain temptations to messing-up for the rest
of our lives, that we must each remember to remember
that we will never be beyond error. Nothing important gets solved once and for all, finally and forever.
The continuing struggle was once described in the
following metaphor by a patient who had successfully
completed a long course of psychotherapy: "I came to
therapy hoping to receive butter for the bread of life.
Instead, at the end, I emerged with a pail of sour milk,
a churn, and instructions on how to use them."

We all remain eternally wandering Jews. Perhaps
all therapy can teach any of us is how to accept the
inevitability of making this unending journey. If Camus
is right, and if knowing that, we do *not* choose suicide,
then how are we to live in a chaotically absurd world
that is so often dominated by human suffering? Perhaps
it calls for the Hasidic commitment to "joy in the world
as it is, in life as it is, in every hour of life in this world,
as that hour is."[7] This means the hallowing of everyday life, taking each experience not as good or as bad,
but as natural. In therapy, this is learned as accepting
my feelings, not because they are constructive, or moral,
or healthy, but simply because they are *mine, here* and
now.

The Pygmies of the Congo know how to accept the darkness of the Great Forest of life:

The complete faith of the Pygmies in the goodness of their forest world is perhaps best of all expressed in one of their great molimo songs, one of the songs that is sung fully only when someone has died. At no time do their songs ask for this or that to be done, for the hunt to be made better or for someone's illness to be cured; it is not necessary. All that is needful is to awaken the forest, and everything will come right. But suppose it does not, supposing that someone dies, then what? Then the men sit around their evening fire . . . and they sing songs of devotion, songs of praise, to wake up the forest and rejoice it, to make it happy again. Of the disaster that has befallen them they sing, in this one great song, "There is darkness all around us; but if darkness *is*, and the darkness is of the forest, then the darkness must be good."[8]

11. Tale of a Journey into the Darkness of the Heart

A civilized European ivory trader, named Kurtz, goes up-river deep into the Congo. There he "degenerates" into a man-god of a primitive native tribe. In order to maintain this ascendancy, which assures his acquiring of ivory, he is "forced" to perform unspeakable rites of human sacifice and cannibalism.

This is the story told by Joseph Conrad in his sinister novella, *Heart of Darkness*.[1] Even at the level of nonsymbolic realistic narrative it is a hauntingly compelling tale. The darkness of the jungle horrors gradually gives way before the curious eye of Marlow, a naïve young opportunist, who follows Kurtz and learns more about himself than he wishes to know.

Watching the wild ritual dancing of the painted Congo savages, his detached curiosity gives way to an uneasy sense of kinship. The worst of it is his growing suspicion that they are *not* inhuman, his gradual fascination with the awareness that he is not so different from them as he first would have liked to believe. As he watched:

> They howled and leaped, and spun, and made horrid faces; but what thrilled you was just the thought of their humanity—like yours—the thought of your remote kinship with this wild and passionate uproar. Ugly. Yes, it was ugly enough; but if you were man enough you would admit to yourself that there was in you just the faintest trace of a response to the terrible frankness of that noise, a dim suspicion of there being a meaning in it which you—you so remote

from the night of the first ages—could comprehend.
And why not?[2]

Psychotherapy patients on their modern spiritual pilgrimage also must become aware of their own kinship
with primitive savagery, with that part of themselves
that society has stamped "unacceptable," of which they
have been *taught to become ashamed*. As children we
owned all of ourselves. As adults, in response to the
expectations of others, we have had to hide much of
ourselves away, out of sight even from our own eyes.
The cost of such voluntary losses is great.

No one can afford to give up any part of himself.
All of you is worth something. Even the evil can be a
source of vitality if only you can face it and transform
it.

Our love of pure goodness, our insistence on innocence, is a hazard. For the sake of appearing to be
what others require us to be, to be more moral than
any man can be, we sacrifice our strength. The pursuit
of the legendary *unicorn* is instructive. Pliny, the Roman
naturalist, described the unicorn as:

a very ferocious beast, similar in the rest of its body
to a horse, with the head of a deer, the feet of an
elephant, the tail of a boar, a deep bellowing voice,
and a single black horn, two cubits in length, standing
out in the middle of its forehead.[3]

The beast was hunted for the powers of its wonderful
horn, which could be used as a virtue against poisons
or be ground up into a potent aphrodisiac powder. So
swift was the unicorn that no man was fast enough to
capture it. Its movable horn was said to be so strong
that if cornered, the unicorn could pitch itself over a
cliff onto it, and walk away unharmed. Pursuit of the
unicorn posed a sad puzzle for its avid hunters.

The unicorn was vulnerable in only one way. It
ever wished to regain its once gentle nature. The beast

insisted on being a great lover of innocence and purity.
So it was that hunters learned to put a young virgin
in its way. The unicorn would approach the maiden,
crouching in reverence, lay his head upon her lap, and
fall into peaceful sleep. At that point the treacherous
virgin could signal the waiting hunters to come and
capture the stubbornly foolish unicorn.

Psychotherapy patients are often foolishly helpless
in the same way. They insist that they are *really* good
(whatever that means). They wish to be rid of any
evil that they may discern in themselves. They talk
of getting over being "sick" or "neurotic" so that they
may then turn to the task of acquiring mental health
and maturity. They find it hard to realize that good is
no more than the other face of evil, that it is all vitality.
"Sin" derives from the old archery term that simply
means "missing the mark."

Patients do not at first realize that they already have
all that they need for a meaningful life. Homosexuality
is heterosexuality gone astray. Hostility is self-assertion
given over to brutality. Passivity is gentleness without
a tender object. My task as guru is to interest the patient in his own evil, so that he may claim and transform it. He must learn to stop fleeing his badness. He
must learn instead to *pursue* the evil urge.

One young woman with whom I worked always
presented herself as sweet, well-intentioned, and helpless. She was the goodest girl imaginable but nothing
ever worked out for her. Her problem was that she
was so easily hurt by the callousness of those around
her. She wanted to be close, and warm, and loving, but
ironically she seemed most often to seek this intimacy
with men who were mean, cold, and unresponsive. No
matter how badly she managed to get treated, she
never showed her vengeful anger except in the form
of pathetic whining and instant tearfulness.

After months of work in a couples-therapy group,
she began to see that despite her never-ending, self-
sorry complaining, she found some safety in the seemingly unrewarding relationship with her impossibly de-

tached husband. Though she experienced me as emotionally open and available, she was not able to feel close to me, either. The absence of self-justifying excuses in *our* relationship reinforced her growing awareness that it was she herself who was maintaining the distance.

One day in the therapy group, I revealed some of my own pain. In response to the touching inner struggle of one of the other patients, I told the group about how difficult it had been for me recently. A serious illness had thrown me back into the turmoil of earlier unresolved emotional problems, and it had been so very hard for me to acknowledge my vulnerability directly enough for me to return to therapy as a patient once more.

A number of the group members were touched, concerned, and sympathetic. But Goodie-Two-Shoes was out of it. She seemed totally unwilling to acknowledge that my troubles could mean anything at all to her. Her only concern was for herself. She stayed back, offered nothing. Any reaching-out on my part was met with harsh, tough-shelled indifference. When I told her what a cold bitch she seemed to me at that moment, she was upset, but only for herself, not for me.

In later individual psychotherapy sessions, she sought the understanding and forgiveness due a little girl who has failed only because what was expected of her was too hard for her to do. I was no longer angry, having already had my say, but now it was I who was totally unmoved by what I experienced as her fraudulent goodness. My continued silence gave her no handle to grab onto. She remained stuck in her conflict, trying to figure out how to be good. After a while, when her efforts to escape seemed spent, I encouraged her to take a fantasy trip into the dark territory from which she was trying to get away.

I had heard all the reasons why she did *not* want to be distant. Now I was curious about what she got out of her avoidance of intimacy. She began, as usual, by talking of her painful vulnerability. When she was younger, she could not even bear to handle flowers, though she loved them. The softness, delicacy, and unbearable fragility of each blossom broke her heart. She could not touch a flower without crying.

Then one day, she discovered that there was one way in which she could experience the loveliness of flowers without feeling the pain. Still-life paintings have remained a great source of pleasure since that time. Her sweet painful response to romantic music soon gave way to the personally less conflictual experience of listening to Baroque music. Her sweet Southern Belle, wide-eyed gentleman-seeking periodically gave way to times when she would deliberately play the controlling seductress, turning men on in situations in which she felt both unmoved and untouchable.

As she was able to get past her mock embarrassment about each of these revelations, I responded with enthusiasm to how much these experiences seemed to mean to her. She became more openly pleased with herself, showing increased self-delight as her tale unfolded. By the time she was telling about instances of explicit cruelty, she was having a ball. In her work, in the guise of taking on administrative responsibility, she was able to degrade and punish other people with impunity. At this point she was no longer kidding herself about *having* to carry out such awful chores. She knew that she looked forward to these opportunities to be sadistic, to inflict pain with impunity, to hurt others from a position of detachment, control, and impervious authority.

In her willingness to expose just how turned on she felt by her cruelty, she came across as more honest, more vivid, and more lively than I had ever experienced her as being up till that point. I told her that it was a relief for me to learn that she was just as capable of evil as I myself am. So that she could experience my malevolence, while yet learning another way to live with evil, I told her of how slavery has always fascinated me.

I abhor the social institution of slavery, would not

participate in it, and am ready to put myself on the line politically to eradicate it. And yet in the secret darkness of my savage heart, I know that I would dig owning slaves. It would be wildly exciting to own another human being, to completely control his destiny, to do what I wished with and to him, to completely have my way with him. I would play out my every self-centered whim on such a hapless object without regard to anyone's pleasure but my own. I like the fact that I can enjoy indulging in such fantasies, not only because of the immediate satisfaction that they afford, but because of the way in which they increase my freedom to live decently. By recognizing this evil in myself, and by satisfying it in fantasy, I decrease the possibilities that I will find some devious ways of living it out with other people. Because I do not pretend that I have no wish to control and degrade another human being, I come to own those wishes, and to be in a position never to express them except by conscious, deliberate, and responsible choice. As a result I am usually free of the temptation to try to manipulate and control others surreptitiously.

It is very important to me that I not hurt other people unless I mean to. Should I choose to strike at another, I wish always to do it purposefully, effectively, and with gusto. I have tried to teach my sons the same freedom and responsibility. I have never struck them except in anger. When each of them was very young, he had the common childhood experience of saying something seemingly innocuous, which turned out to be deeply hurtful to someone else. I took considerable time and effort to help him to become more sensitive to the feelings of others, to learn what words caused undue pain. I encouraged him to take care to avoid hurting people needlessly, carelessly, unintentionally, to learn to give something of himself to understanding how other people felt. But I also tried to teach him that the other face of this sensitivity to how other people feel—the other face of this loving goodness—would be the power of controlled evil. He could keep his sharply

honed, well-tamed anger in his pocket most of the
time, but he must remember to take it out when he
needs it. To allow another person to do him in is to be
accomplice to the other's destructiveness in the name
of one's own prideful, pietistic "goodness." I have
taught my sons to love, but first of all I have tried to
teach them how to hate openly when need be so that
they may survive.

And too, by exposing my own ambiguously good/
bad nature to them, I have tried to help them to live
with the universally human impurity of their own motives. None of us ever seem to operate out of pure
goodness. But being less than perfect can be its own
kind of fun. I have tried to help my sons to find their
own inner selves more acceptable to each of them by
freely and unashamedly revealing my own base feelings.
I am not what society has taught me that I ought to be.
As far as I can tell, neither is anyone else.

Most recently my being seriously ill has again put
me in close touch with my malice. At first I only wished
my illness to be put off onto some bad person. "Adolph
Hitler should only have my troubles," my mother used
to say. But when things got really bad, I would have
been delighted to transfer my pain to someone else,
regardless of his worth, to anyone else other than myself. And too, I know and savor in myself my envy of
others' good fortune (even when in the main I can feel
the generosity of my joy for their happiness). The bad
luck, suffering, and even the death of an enemy always
gives me a sense of well-being. It is a time to cele-
brate.

In truth, to me all of this seems neither good nor
bad, so much as simply natural. Like it or not, it is
the way I am. It is best for me that I find what I can
for myself in my inconsistent, so very fallible nature.
In therapy, a patient can learn to become aware of the
evil in himself, to live with it as he can, enjoy it as he
may, and forgive himself for being human. In the
closing monologue of his autobiographical play, *After*

the Fall, Arthur Miller reviews his calamitous relationships with women. They have been good and warm and exciting, but they have always had elements of destructiveness in them as well. In the face of his awareness of the inevitable evil in himself and in the world, he struggles with how to go on living with this self in such a world. He knows that people will go on hurting each other, one way or another. This is the knowledge that comes with the Fall of man. What are we to do with the recognition of our own evil? Miller asks:

> Is the knowing all? To know, and even happily, that we meet unblessed; not in some garden of wax fruit and painted trees, that lies East of Eden, but after, after the Fall, after many, many deaths. Is the knowing all? . . . And the wish to kill is never killed, but with some gift of courage one may look into its face when it appears, and with a stroke of love—as to an idiot in the house—forgive it; again and again . . . forever?[4]

It seems to me that the greater problem belongs to those who turn away, who will not look unblinkingly into the darkness of their own hearts. Inhuman catastrophes such as the Holocaust, the Nazi extermination of the Jews, come about *not* because of the immense evil of one man-beast, such as the unbelievable monstrosity of Adolph Hitler. Such horrors are possible not because of the *evil* of one man, but because of the *folly* of the many. Because so many men will not face the darkness of their own hearts, a few can wreak havoc on the rest of us.

If facing the individual evil in each of us can prevent further social horrors, that would be reward enough. But there is something of purely personal importance to be gained by anyone who will not turn away from the darkness of his own heart. In Conrad's tale, Marlow turns back short of realizing full awareness of his secret self. At the journey's end, when it is too late to

complete his personal pilgrimage, Marlow compares
his own flinching failure of nerve with Kurtz's willingness to go all the way.

> True, he had made that last stride, he had stepped over
> the edge, while I had been permitted to draw back my
> hesitating foot. And perhaps in this is the whole differ-
> ence; perhaps all the wisdom, and all truth, and all
> sincerity are just compressed into that inappreciable
> moment of time in which we step over the threshold
> of the invisible. Perhaps! I like to think my summing-
> up would not have been a word of careless contempt.
> Better his cry [The horror! The horror!]—much
> better. It was an affirmation, a moral victory paid for
> by innumerable defeats, by abominable terrors, by
> abominable satisfactions. But it was a victory.[5]

Part Three: Fragments of the Education of a Fool

In the telling of the tales thus far, I have cast myself as Guru, as Guide, as Most Experienced Pilgrim. Now I would reveal the stumbling novice I once was when first I began the pilgrimage that is my work. And so it is that these three tales are fragments of the education of a fool.

Half a lifetime ago, as a very young man and a largely unseasoned psychotherapist, I came in arrogance as a patronizing visitor to a Building for the Criminally Insane. My patients were to be those shamefully uncontrolled pariahs known as Sex Offenders. I came to teach them how to live, and stayed long enough to learn from them. I came to guide them. Most often I failed. But at times, as we traveled together, we helped one another. It is not clear to me, even now, whether I ever gave to them as much as they gave to me.

1. Who Cares?

Norman always reminded me of a white mouse I had as a child. Perhaps it was Norman's deadly pale complexion, relieved only by the redness around his eyes and nose (which also served to suggest a perpetual head cold). I knew that Norman was taller and weighed more than my mouse, but Norman did always seem almost that much smaller than anyone else in the therapy group. His manner contributed to the image as well.

I didn't know about other people's mice, but mine had had only two moods. The first was one of contentment, though it was hard for most people to distinguish it from simple apathy. At such times he could be petted or prodded, dangled by the tail or rolled into a ball, all without any apparent sign of overt disturbance. Most of the time, Norman, too, met all questions, reassurances, and abuses with bland compliance and an unchanging excuse for a smile, which lacked any genuine gaiety.

My mouse's only other alternative attitude appeared in the form of episodic moments of seemingly unwarranted panic. They came without warning or apparent cause as though precipitated from within, and were expressed in short, darting movements, which seemed to lack purpose but somehow spoke of a need to escape (but from what inner source of terror?). His whiskers twitched, his eyes blazed, and a fine tremor ran along the length of his body. At such times, he always looked as if he would involuntarily empty his bowels, and often did. Norman lacked only the whiskers and the final loss of sphincter control.

Norman was what is known in the mental health trade as "flat." That is, he had the emotional emptiness of a burned-out, back-ward schizophrenic. He could say, "I guess I always wanted to kill my brother," with the same bland absence of intensity as when he told us, "We always had eggs for breakfast."

This is perhaps clearer when you consider the fact that to Norman it was a matter of complete indifference what he had for breakfast or whether he had it at all. Partly, it was this dehumanized quality, this lack of vitality that made it so hard for me to develop sufficient concern for Norman. More important than that was that my sarcasm was an angry answer to Norman as a disappointing patient whose indifference defeated my every despairing attempt at therapeutic intervention. I had always found a touch of this unkind attitude arising with such burned-out cases, even when I had no therapeutic responsibility for them. Such patients had always made me uneasy. They had the quality of animated but lifeless mannequins, lacking the vitality and spark of fire to be found in even the most pedestrian normals. Sometimes when I was with such a patient, my own human spirit seemed unreal. At such times I felt like the explorer of a childhood adventure story who has been given a choice by the mad scientist, either to become a zombie or to live among them as he is. He chooses the latter alternative in hope of escaping, only to find himself shouting at them, hitting at them, making desperate attempts to elicit a human response from them. At last (some time before his inevitable rescue) he decides he has made the wrong choice. His own panicky rantings seem less real than the expressionless indifference of the zombies.

This inability to really care about a patient no longer happens as often, but when it does, I still feel ashamed. Back then it seemed that the magic cloak of my therapist's role could never hide my limitations as a person, nor from the patients, nor from my colleagues, and least of all from myself. In an abstract way I knew that men like Norman must have suffered beyond belief or they never would have ended up so apparently devoid of human feelings. Only pains of life too intense to be borne could lead a man to forgo all response, to give up completely the joy of living as other men live.

In an attempt somehow to get through the barrier of Norman's apathy (or of my own insensitivity), I reviewed the hospital medical chart to find those events in Norman's history that would tie him to other men. Perhaps this could make him come alive at least in my experience. After all, Norman wasn't born at forty-four. He came to this point down paths that other men had trod. His chart would certainly establish this, as well as revealing him as a unique individual in his own way.

This is what I found.

Norman _____. Born January 5, 1911. Delivery normal. Usual childhood diseases. Completed 8th grade. Intelligence considered to be within normal limits. Job history sporadic, mostly unskilled. Community activities limited to voluntary Sunday School teaching. Never married, never dated. Parents born in Germany. Father died of influenza when patient was six years old. Mother dull, invalided, cause unknown. Two older brothers, both more successful in school and employment. Neither married. All three were living at home at time of patient's most recent arrest. Patient has been described by those who knew him as shy, seclusive, quiet, cooperative, and placid.

The present offense was not the first, and five prior charges were quite similar. Previous arrests resulted in two dismissals on the basis of insufficient evidence, a two hundred dollar fine, a one-year term in the county workhouse and another five-year term in the State prison.

There were other such acts in the intervening years to which Norman later admitted, but he had not been found out again for several years. By the time of his current arrest, the State legislature had succumbed to the enlightened lobbying of local psychiatrists, mental health organizations and other such groups, and so Norman was sentenced under the new Psychiatric Sexual Offender Law. There had been a good deal of opposition to this statute, emphasizing as it did therapy and rehabilitation of patients, rather than punishment and deterrence of criminal perverts. The resistance of the God-fearing, right-living citizenry was overcome in part because the neighboring state had recently passed its own such statute. Competition for the achievement of "the most progressive government in the Northeast" was an important moral force.

This complex of pressures resulted in some strange paradoxes. Thus, though Norman was committed to a mental hospital for psychiatric treatment rather than being resentenced to the prison for punitive incarceration, his charge read:

> Indictment 296 recites that Norman _____ on the 21st day of June 1954 in the city of Ridgeville, with force and arms, in and upon one Catherine _____, a female child under the age of 16 years, then and there being, feloniously did make an assault and then and there feloniously, wickedly, diabolically, and against the order of nature, had a venereal affair with the said Catherine _____ and then and there feloniously, wickedly and diabolically and against the order of nature, with the said Catherine _____ did commit and perpetrate the destestable and abominable crime of sodomy, not to be named among Christians, to the great displeasure of the Almighty God, to the great scandal of all humankind, against the peace of this State Government and the dignity of the same, and furthermore, contrary to the provisions of the State Statute No. 7A: 154-3.

The medical chart went on to a brief psychiatric evaluation which said of Norman:

> Sensorium clear; no hallucinations or delusions elicited; alcoholism, drugs and suicidal attempts denied; emotionally flat; thinking vague and confused,

seclusive and withdrawn; no sense of guilt with regard to history of sexually molesting pre-pubertal girls. Diagnostic Impression: Schizophrenic Reaction, Chronic Undifferentiated Type.

All in all, reviewing the medical chart did little for me to make Norman come alive or to waken the concern for him which I had hoped to feel.

In the group I hoped that perhaps if I could get Norman to relive his offenses, step by step, it would become clear just what feelings had driven him to commit the crime. And so, after much coaxing, Norman told the group about Catherine:

She was very pretty, blonde hair and all. And slim. I like them slim. The fat ones look too old and feel too soft. She used to come around the drug store where I went to look at the magazines, you know, the picture ones. She had lots of good ideas, and we'd tell our opinions and stuff about the pictures. After a while she let me buy her a soda. I was really getting to like her, her being so smart and all.

Then one day I brought my camera and asked how she'd like to go to the woods and take some pictures. She said, "Yeah," right away and I knew she had a crush on me, too. I wondered if she thought of me at night, you know, like I thought of her. Well, anyway, when we got to the woods, I didn't try nothing fresh or nothing . . . least not right off. You know, girls don't like that the first time they go someplace with you. I worked up kind of real easy. First, I talked to her about how we liked the same things and all, and how smart I thought she was. She liked that part.

And then, like I always did before I'd try anything, I started supposing. You know, like supposing a fella kissed her, how would she like it? And then supposing the fella was a guy like me. And then supposing it *was* me. All easy like. And she said she *would* like it, so I kissed her. And then after a while, I just kind of supposed her into taking her panties off so I could rub her. And then I even got to put it in for a while you

know, in the back. And she really liked it. Didn't hurt
or nothing, she said. We played around for a long
time, too long, I guess. That's why her mother got to
asking her about it. And then her folks got mad and
scared her away from me. They wanted to break it up
between us, so they got me put in jail.

The group was stunned, and some were appalled by
the quiet, unashamed way in which Norman told the
story. It was recited with no more intensity than the
nostalgia of a long ago love affair, no longer painful,
but still wistfully remembered. At no point did Norman seem impressed by the fact that he himself was
well into his forties, while Catherine was only *nine
years old*.

Norman's session, if it can be called that, did not
come until almost a year later. It was a long year for
me. There was really no discernible change in Norman through those many months. I found myself paying less and less attention to him. My repertoire of
therapeutic gambits, calculated to draw a man out,
had long been exhausted, withering as they did into
impotent ineffectuality before the terrible onslaught of
Norman's vigorous apathy. The other men, too, often
ignored Norman, or even seemed annoyed when he
awakened enough to comment with ingenuous irrele-
vance. They no longer even tried to tease him because
his vacuously sincere gratitude for their attention made
them feel mildly guilty.

Perhaps that's why no one noticed that Norman
had not uttered a single word during the previous few
sessions. It was during the time when Ross and Jimmy
were probing the roots of their homosexuality, and
discussing in vivid detail just what went on in their
bodies and their minds during lovemaking. No one
would have expected Norman to be any more moved
by this than by all the other feelings and experiences,
which had been grist for the therapeutic mill. Perhaps
I should have seen it coming, but I didn't. Norman
was as lost to me as he had been to all of the other

people in his empty life who might have cared enough to help him.

Norman had never taken it on himself to begin a session before. But it was not only this untoward spontaneity that captured everyone's attention. It was the *way* he spoke. There was a new pressure driving his words from between tension-whitened lips and a tautness to his tone like a stringed instrument tuned just a bit too high. And he spoke with an increased volume of which he was apparently unaware, as though the others were a bit too far away for a conversational tone.

"You know that fairy stuff you guys been talking got me thinking. I mean really thinking . . . and *watching.*"

The men were obviously uncomfortable and tried to kid Norman back into character. "You don't want to think too hard, Normie boy, it'll hurt your brain."

But he ignored their jibes and went on, his voice suddenly dropping to a whisper. "It's these young colored punks, mainly. You know, if they get to play with a white guy's thing, that's quite a feather in their cap."

I smelled the foul stench of psychosis, the internal rotting and decay of thoughts and feelings. "This is pretty disturbing to you, Norman, isn't it?"

But Norman went on. "No. No. I'm smarter than a *lot* of guys think I am. I know just how to take care of old Norm. Don't think I don't. They weren't supposed to be out of their cells at night. You know that's a rule here, isn't it, Doc?"

"That's right, Norman. That's a rule here," I answered. It was meant to be reassuring, but my voice was dulled by resignation and quiet melancholy.

The other men understood my sadness and were quite still after that.

Norman went on, as much to himself as to anyone else. "Don't you worry, I heard them. It's me they been talking about, for a week now. It's kind of a code, secret, like spies. But I hear them say, 'His ass, his ass.' So I know what they want all right. But they're not gonna do that to me. Not to old Norm."

He suddenly and inexplicably became enraged. "And no sucking, either. No sucking. Do you get that?" he screamed.

And then, quietly again, and with great cleverness glinting in his eyes, "But you guys can just stop your worrying, 'cause I'm gonna cut them all up. Can't touch old Norm if they're all cut up in pieces, can they? Sometimes I think I should kill myself instead, then they'd never get me nohow. But don't worry, Doctor. I'll try my best not to hurt myself nor nobody, if they just leave me be. I know you don't like that, and you're my friend. So, maybe I'll just hide out for a while. They know I'm up here in sex class now, so maybe I could trick them by going down and hiding in my cell. Can I go down now and hide, Doc, can I?"

"Yes, Norman," I replied. "Ask the attendant to take you down to your cell. Tell him I said it's okay. You'll be safe there, Norman, I promise." My attempt at great gentleness was somewhat impaired by my even greater weariness.

Norman got up, obviously pleased with his plan. His steps down the tier were purposefully stealthy as he peered out of the corners of his eyes into each empty cell as he passed.

The group and I spent the remainder of the hour discussing with concern whether or not Norman would get better. We knew we had failed him, and ourselves.

After the hour, I reported the incident to the psychiatrist-in-charge. Norman was given a short course of shock therapy. After he had recovered from his postshock bewilderment, I stopped in to visit him.

Now I cared, now that it was too late. The other men in group mourned Norman as they might a handicapped brother who had died, a child lost somehow because no one knew how to ask him where it hurt.

2. The Land and the Sea

Until I heard Ross's story, I had never been very much moved by past descriptions of the beatings that other men had endured as children. A beating is at least an honest, open, often impersonal statement to the child. Painful, yes, but the hurt diminishes as time passes.

The many times when I had been hit as punishment for misbehaving, I could always tell when it was unfair. Once that was clear I could hate back and rebel in a way that left me feeling clean and free. The more frequent mode in my own home were times when the wages of sin were having to sit and listen to heartrending tales of parental sacrifices and of children's ingratitudes. The seeds of guilt were so well sown that the harvests of anxiety were reaped more and more richly in each season of a man's life. The uncontrollable yields were halted, or at least diminished, only when, with the help of my own therapist, I painfully dug up the entire field so that I could plant my own crop.

Even now, so many years later, remembering the story raises the hairs on the back of my neck and arms, bringing back the old empty, helpless feeling, which seems to be in both my throat and the pit of my stomach at the same time. It was told and retold to the children, in English, or in Yiddish, or in some arbitrary combination of the two. It was told at a time when Momma was feeling concerned that the children did not appreciate how much of a treasure they had in her love. When she was a child it had been different. Then they knew what a mother was, and they were so grateful they got down on their knees to thank God for this treasure. But in your America, what is a mother? Dirt under the feet of the children, children whom she had borne in pain. "A blessing on Columbus," she would say. She meant, of course, a curse on this goy who had started all the trouble, but this way you knew it, but she never said it.

Then it would come. Momma always began with her version of a rhetorical question (or at least one that she quickly answered herself lest her ungrateful children provide the wrong response). "You know what a mother is? So, I'll tell you what a mother is. A mother is love, and suffering, and you have only one, and you won't know what she's worth till it's time to sit shivva and mourn for her. And then, it will be too late. Wait, I'll tell you a story of what a mother goes through for her children's happiness." At this point her voice invariably took on the sing-song rhythm and lilt of the synagogue liturgy. She always told the story as though we had never heard it before.

Once, a long time ago, it could be anytime, a mother is mother no matter when. . . . So, once, at some time in the past, there lived a poor widowed Jewish mother and her son. By herself, she raised him. He was not a bad boy, but when he was eighteen, he fell in love with a shicksa. Plenty of nice Jewish girls there were in his village. His poor mother told him to stay with his own kind, but youth is deaf and blind and foolish. So . . . what can I tell you? These things happen. It came to pass that he fell in love with this beautiful shicksa, the unthinking love of the young.

His mother, of course, knew he was troubled (a mother always knows) but she did not know the reason because this foolish boy did not confide in her. Now the shicksa was not serious about the boy, fool that she was. She only played with him. What can you expect from a Christian head? At last she tired of him. This was his chance to escape back to his mother. But a boy, a fool, what he cannot have, that he must have.

He told the girl he would do anything she asked, anything, if only she would marry him.

At last, to be done with him forever, the shicksa made a terrible covenant with him, knowing he would never fulfill it. Not even a goy would ask this in seriousness. But she did not know the fire of this boy's foolish infatuation. She told him . . . she told him . . . I can hardly bring myself to tell you . . . , she said to him, "I will marry you only if you cut out your mother's heart and bring it to me. Only this way can you prove your love." The boy was filled with horror. To kill his own mother. . . . Yet, he must have this forbidden girl. And so he stole into his own house like a thief in the night. And in the dark of night he knelt beside the bed in which his mother slept the sleep of the good. He knelt and prayed that the Lord God would understand and forgive him for what he must do. And so, this ungrateful boy took from his belt a knife from his mother's kitchen, and plunged it into the breast of his poor sleeping mother. He killed her and cut out her heart. He could feel the warmth of her heart in his blood-stained hands as he rushed from their home to the house of his shicksa. As he ran up the cobblestoned street of their village, with the heart of his mother clutched in his guilty hands, he stumbled and almost fell.

And, as he stumbled, he heard the voice of his mother's heart speak to him from his hands. His mother's heart said, "Be careful, my son."

That is a mother's love.[1]

At first I had rarely connected the patients' childhood problems with my own. I knew that their neuroses led them to exaggerate and to distort, but sympathy for the patients sometimes led me to participate in their fantasies. Part of their illness was, of course, that they maintained a view of their parents that had originated when they were helpless children, when parents were giants by virtue of the child's complete dependence on them. I have always liked to think of this perspective as "a disadvantage point." That's why it was so helpful when, in meeting the parents and seeing what sort of people they really were, I could dispel the distortions born of the patient's neurosis.

Learning of her visit, I wondered what Ross's foster mother would be like. Ross had always talked of his mother with anger and bitterness but also with a kind of resignation in the face of the great power that he mistakenly ascribed to her. I knew from the social worker's careful case history of Ross that his stepmother was a retired seamstress, an ailing woman of almost sixty. I looked forward to being able to report my impression of this little old lady to the group in an attempt to help Ross to a more realistic evaluation of her. In this way, Ross would be able to recognize that for all these years he had been intimidated by his own distorted perceptions and that a grown man need no longer fear an aging stepmother whose health was failing.

Because of this, I did not mind staying late at the hospital. That was as it should be. I did not want my frustration at having to delay my supper to lead me to be short with this poor woman. She had come so far because of her sorrow over her son's imprisonment. As I awaited her knock, I thought to myself, "I must be very gentle with her." But the knock never came. Instead, the door burst open as if before a heavy wind that suddenly introduces a destructive storm. And then came the storm in the form of a huge woman whose steel-grey head and massive shoulders thrust forward through the doorway carrying the rest of her bulk behind her. She was dressed severely and well-girdled, though less in a way suggesting some concern with femininity than in a manner that reminded me of the armor plating so necessary to the most efficient functioning of a Sherman Tank.

She wielded a large, unadorned, black leather pocketbook, which swayed menacingly over my head as she screeched to a halt before my desk, and followed her outstretched arm with the accusation, "You're Dr. Kopp." Acknowledging my guilt, I tremblingly await- ed sentencing, but found that first I had to sit through a detailed description of my crimes. At no time was I allowed to interrupt in my own defense, though I tried to do so at several junctures. The indictment ran as follows:

I had to come all this way on a hot train, almost three dollars round trip, and me with a heart condition. It's people like you who make other people miserable. Don't give me that business about how you're just doing your job either. My Rossey shouldn't be here in the first place. A good boy thrown in with those hardened criminals. If he really does get into any trouble after I get him out of here his crime will be on your head. The filth, the terrible food. I'm sure he doesn't get his greens and he's a very fussy eater. He was a very thin child. No, don't tell me about it. I'm a taxpayer and someday the rest of them will get wise to all of you. Now, who do I see about this? Who's your boss? I want my Rossey released immediately or at least put in a cleaner part of the hospital. In there with all those murderers and thieves, and worse. No, I don't want to hear anything about those lies they told about Rossey in court. You don't know him or you could never believe all that filth. It's none of it true. How could it be? Just you take a look at how meticulous his clothes are, always neat and clean. He never missed a bath one night in my home since I took him in when he was eight years old. So you just go ahead and tell me how he could have done any of those disgusting things they said in court. No, don't you dare repeat them. I'm a good Christian woman. I haven't gone to church every week to hear you repeat all that foul- mouthed filth you psychiatrists study.

This went on and on with my attempts at interrup- tion growing more and more feeble. When I finally arranged an appointment for her with the hospital's clinical director, I did so with anger and bitterness, but also with a kind of resignation in the face of the great power I had met in her.

This meeting made Ross's experience more real to me. At first it had been difficult to imagine Ross in the role of a seducer of young boys. He certainly did not look the part. He was tall and rangy, with powerful chest, and long, slim, muscular arms swinging freely with the roll of the deck his feet never seemed to have left. The title, "able-bodied seaman," suited him, and there was much of the old salt in his easy-flowing, exaggerated tales of far-off ports and never-ending seas. He had about him a cynicism that did not so much reject the land as demand that the land know its place. He was thus not only a man, but a voyager who might be expected to have left women remembering him in many ports of call. Yet and still, his voice would fill with tenderness and emotion only when he told of some "beautiful child" whom he had found wandering the streets, ill-fed and uncared for. He told of them going through the port markets and bazaars until he found some exactly right compass or telescope such as would fill the boy with wonder and excitement. Having thus captivated the boy, he would take him to eat as much as he could hold of whatever he wanted, buy him the clothes he most admired, give him more money than he had ever possessed, and then take him to a furnished room. Once in the room, he would take the boy on his lap and say, "Now, I would like you to let me love you. If you don't want this, you may leave. But whether you stay or go, you may keep all that I have given to you. And whether you stay or go, I shall never give you anything more; no food, no money, no presents. If you stay, it will be only because you want to let me love you." He insisted that very few of the boys left, and so he knew for sure that many wanted his love. He always described these encounters as his "hours of truth." It was months later before it came to light that very few of the three boys understood English, the only language he spoke.

In earlier years the bulk of these affairs took place only when his ship docked in foreign ports. Though there were no women on board the freighters that he sailed, he'd somehow never sought a sexual partner from among his shipmates. Instead, he spent his leisure time reading, keeping a diary of his fantasies, and arguing his own kind of crude and cynical metaphysics with anyone whom he could bait or otherwise engage.

And when his ship was in port, he would usually begin his shore leave by searching for a woman, and sometimes even finding one to share his bed. But very soon there would arise the matter of the trinket. His foster mother, the only mother he had ever known, was certainly appreciative of the money he sent her. But if he was really a good boy, he must also send her a trinket, some small bauble, to show that he would never forget her no matter how far off the foreign port in which he landed. Somehow, being with, or even looking for a woman of the streets, would bring this obligation to mind. Strange how remembering his promise to this angry woman of God, who had raised him on Bible-readings and belt-lashings, should unfailingly arise whenever he was with some hedonistic tramp, for whom he could be any man with money. Never a Magdalene without a Madonna to spoil it. Perhaps it was the contrast, as though for him memory was guided by some strange law of opposites.

As much as he had always bitterly resented mother, she did want to save him from . . . from Hellfire and Damnation, she said. Perhaps this meant from the very women he sought in these dark places so far from her harsh light. And in a sense, perhaps she had. Thoughts of her never failed to sour the sweetness of his lust. He was left with little more than disgust with the woman, with himself, with the secret things they did together. Sometimes he tried to push back this feeling, but it only gagged and sickened him all the more, choking off the desire that would have made him potent and a man. It was at such times that he would find himself a beautiful child.

During the year before his arrest, some undiagnosed illness, some vague aching and fever, had kept him from shipping out once more. For the first time in many years he lived once more under the discomforting judgment of his foster mother's righteous eye. Now he found that his need for young boys arose more and more often, with a growing intensity, which crowded out his usual cautiousness. At last, as had to happen, one boy became frightened and told his parents of what the man had done to him and made him do.

It was his arrest for this encounter that had brought Ross to this therapy group. Through the many months of treatment, Ross seemed a strange admixture of concealment and candor. He was often quite open in his concern for the other men's pain and unhappiness, but whenever this was pointed out or met with appreciation, he quickly became distant or snarlingly sarcastic. At first the others were hurt and angry, or frankly bewildered. Only slowly did they come to understand. And strangely enough in some secret way Ross appeared to enjoy the fact that they were wise to him, that they accepted a softness in him that he could not himself acknowledge.

So, too, he would not talk about himself with any real seriousness. When questioned, he often evaded by opening his sea chest of tales, which he warned them in advance not to believe. At other times he would volunteer satirical bits of alleged autobiography. These episodes were so broadly exaggerated that they could not be regarded as more than half-truths, yet the very nature of the distortions disclosed more than they hid. These included, for example, a long, elaborately "scientific" story of his efforts as a boy to train his dog to bite his mother's hand when she fed him. He interrupted the men's laughter to assure them that all of this was "Gospel truth," just before ending the story with the dog running off yelping, never to be seen again, because his mother had bitten the dog first. Despite all of this banter, however, he often went on to admit that this was all a "smoke screen," behind which lay feelings too frightening to reveal.

Some weeks before Ross's session, I had pushed him hard about his use of sea stories to hold off the group, even as he had used the sea to separate himself from his mother. How ironic that he had failed to escape from her dangerous storming, while he might well succeed in protecting himself from the safe harbor offered by these men who had grown to care for him. The depth of Ross's disturbance was perhaps best expressed in his pleading with me. "Don't take the sea away from me. I can't let you. It's all I've got left. There'll be no place else to hide and then I'll know how empty I am inside." The other men met this plea by describing the risks they had faced in leaving their own fortresses, the protection of alcohol, toughness, compliance, and the like. These confessions had a directness that moved Ross in spite of himself.

From that hour onward, he told a good deal about himself, blurting out his battered feelings with frantic, pressured speech, as though he could not tell fast enough and dared not tarry lest he not tell it all. He told of how he had longed for his father. At each age he created new tales, so well told that his schoolmates envied him the absent father who so much dwarfed their own. Actually, all he ever knew for sure was that his father had shipped out on a freighter only weeks before his birth. He did not remember his natural mother either and recalled his years at the orphanage only vaguely. His foster mother would not say more than that she had been a bad woman, and Ross was fortunate that the good Lord had allowed him this Christian home with someone to raise him right. She was all the mother he was going to have, and he'd better get down on his knees and thank God for giving him better than he deserved. If he asked about his parents, he was not answered but punished for being an ungrateful little sinner.

It was this punishment about which he began to talk

on the day of his session. Many of the other men had been knocked about a good deal themselves and were unwilling to allow him much sympathy on the grounds of physical punishment alone.

I, too, was uninspired. I so much preferred the simple beatings to what I more often had endured as a child. It was not until I heard Ross out that I knew that it was not so much whether or not a child was beaten that was important. Instead it depended on what the punishment came to mean to him that determined whether it just hurt on the outside or went on tearing at his guts even when he was supposed to have become a man.

The other men encouraged Ross to go on with the story left unfinished at the end of the last hour. And so he did, speaking slowly and quietly, but through almost clenched teeth. "When I'd ask about my folks, she'd reach into her apron pocket for the length of sewing machine strap she always kept there. Then she'd start. It was kind of slow at first. Each lick she'd give me she would find another way of saying how sinful and ungrateful I was. The more excited she'd become the faster she'd swing that strap. She'd go on and on. She beat me until I'd scream, but that wasn't the worst." He paused for a long moment, licking slowly at his parched lips. "After that she'd keep on beating me until I stopped screaming. God, it was hard to stop sometimes. . . . And then, once I'd settled down to just whimpering, she'd make me come over to her and tell her that I loved her and was sorry for being so ungrateful to the only good mother God gave me."

There were groans of pain from every man in the group and gasps of "what a thing to do to a kid" and "you poor bastard." Ross paused, breathing deeply, and then began again. "I hated her, man, how I hated her." Then on, with a desperately lighter tone, "I even tried to kill her once. Yeah. I put moth crystals in her tea, but she didn't even taste it, and I didn't have the nerve to try it again. But that's all behind me now. Oh sure, I wanted to kill her, you know, like a kid feels like doing. Moth crystals, can you imagine that? Only now I'm grown and things are different."

"Are they really any different . . . inside?" I asked.

Ross tried to throw this off lightly, but I persisted and so did some of the men. They saw the way Ross clenched his teeth, hunched forward, and gripped the chair with whitening fingers, and they gave him the lie. After a few exchanges, they continued, but he stopped answering. When at last he sprang from his seat, the group met him with sudden silence and apprehension. They could see the crazy look in his eyes.

He moved slowly, heavily, toward me. "I want your chair, and I'm going to have it," he croaked hoarsely. Whether though fear or wisdom I rose quickly and stepped aside. I thought, "God, how he needs this chair. He would kill me for it." But to Ross, I only answered softly, "Sure, if you want it that badly, Ross, you can have it."

For a moment, Ross looked beaten and disappointed. Then, as he seemed to fill with strength, he stepped forward, grasping the heavy backrest of my empty chair. As he lifted the chair above his head, there were frightened gasps, but no one moved. Ross seemed to be off somewhere inside his own head as he stepped away from the group, moved in slow motion toward the bars of the nearest cell, and then brought the chair down and forward with great and sudden force. Though splintering of wood crashing against steel bars should have brought everyone to life, still no one moved.

I found myself strangely detached from all this. The fear and the trembling were not to come until later, at another place and another time. For the moment, I found myself speculating casually as if about some improbably hypothetical situation. It all seemed very far away. At the first splintering crash, I wondered vaguely if Ross were trying to break the chair down to some handy size with which to batter me. And then, as the banging and clanging rang and resounded up and down the long stone and steel corridors of the prison, from some still greater distance, I wondered first how much such a chair would cost to replace, and then, whether they would deduct the cost from my already inadequate salary.

After what seemed a long and loud and endless angry time of it, the many pieces of the chair lay like silence, scattered about Ross's widespread feet. With the total fragmenting of the chair, so too did his rage at last seem spent. He slouched forward, arms dangling at his side, done in, exhausted.

At this, the whole group seemed to unwind from their long state of tense immobility, as though assured they would not be punished or deprived any more than Ross would.

"Funny," Ross said to me, "all the time I was smashing that chair, I kept thinking I'd have to gather up the pieces and take them back to my cell with me."

"But now you don't need to. Who needs a broken up old chair, a chair that was never any comfort to begin with?"

"Yeah. Another thing, I'm real glad you didn't try to stop me. You're a good guy really. Maybe the only one who understands, everything, I mean. I don't want to hurt you in any way. Yet, when I went for the chair, in some crazy way, I wanted to have the chance to fight you for it. Crazy, huh?"

"Maybe you got mixed up with your mother for a while there."

Ross nodded. Now the group began to respond, first with nervous laughter and tension-dispelling wisecracks. Then they settled down to seriously explaining what all of this meant. They explained this mainly to each other, because Ross and I didn't listen very hard. We didn't have to. We both knew, each in his own way.

Ross did not talk very much about his mother in the months that followed. But now his tenderness toward the other men was an open, proud and blossoming thing, and he was happy when the others recognized how it was with him. Eventually, a short while before his release, he began to talk longingly about a young woman he had known, a widow left with two small kids when her husband was drowned at sea. I never did find out how it all worked out. Ross never called or wrote once he hit the streets. Yet, I felt that it might well be better for him, as it was then getting better for me.

All this time, the white-jacketed attendants had been piling up behind the locked grill gate at the end of the long corridor. Only now did those bastards unlock the door and rush heroically to my rescue. I came painfully alive at the same moment and waved them off in disgust. Suddenly I felt very close to Ross and as exhausted as if I too had spat forth my fury.

Ross stumbled back to his own chair and carried it clumsily to where I stood. "Here, Doctor Kopp, take mine," he panted.

"Thank you," I answered softly, as I settled tiredly into Ross's chair.

Ross, himself, then collapsed to the floor like a puppet whose strings had been cut, and pulled himself up to a sitting position against the stone wall. He looked somehow older, and so very tired. For a moment, his eyes blazed once more as he said fiercely, "I'm going to stay till the end. This is my session, and I get to finish it. After that they can lock me up, but not till it's over."

I found a new calmness in myself as I replied, "You can stay, Ross. It's going to be okay. I sent them away."

3. Some for Him and Some for Me[1]

The attendant on the wing unlocked the isolation cell's great steel door. I pushed it open to find the new inmate resting on a wooden chair, which had been tilted back to lean against the cell wall as if he were sunning himself. The man's unconvincing smile spread only to one side of his mouth in a half-hearted way, and his raggedly sleeveless shirt revealed muscular arms folded in an air of casual defiance. He did not get up, nor even lean forward when I entered.

"Good morning. My name is Dr. Kopp. You're Anthony Dellini?"

"Yeah, Little Tony D. Come to bug me out, Doc?"

"I want to get to know you, Anthony. Maybe I can help."

"Yeah. What's chances of a parole? The judge, he told me I get a chance in six months. That's why I said okay to going to the bug house instead of State Prison."

"Men sentenced under the sex offender law are considered every six months, but they can keep you the whole fifteen years. The staff doesn't have to let you out till they think you're ready to go out."

"Fifteen years, Bafongu. I was ready to get out the first day I got in. No shit, Doc. I got to get out. I got three kids. The little guy, Dominick, he's smart, but he won't listen to nobody but me. His mother's too soft and too dumb. He's like me."

"You wouldn't listen to anyone but your father either?"

"My old man. Jeez, he's old country. He don't know

172

what's coming off anywhere outside of Sicily. Me, listen to him—nah. I didn't listen to nobody."

"How come, Tony?"

"They was always telling me, 'Be a good boy.' My brothers, they could get away with anything. I ain't gonna be a good boy to get out of here, either. You can be a man and still get a parole, can't you?"

"You get out—if we know you won't get into trouble again."

"Get into trouble, ay, what trouble? This thing was a frame-up. This girl only said I raped her 'cause she was jealous. She wanted me to mess with her. Bothered me for weeks. Only I wouldn't."

"You wouldn't mess with her because you were married?"

"No, man, 'cause she was a dog. That broad was so ugly that . . ."

"How is it that she was able to convince the jury?"

"I didn't have no jury. That crummy shyster got me to plead noli . . . noli something."

"Noli me contendere. That means you didn't contest the case. You didn't claim to be innocent in court."

"Yeah, that bastard said I had no defense 'cause I was so looped I couldn't remember what happened that night. I remember she came over to talk to me while I was sitting in my car, downing a pint. But that's all. Man, I was stoned."

"Then you don't really know that you didn't rape her."

"What's a matter. . . . No, I guess I don't."

"Tell me more about the trouble you had getting along with your family."

"I didn't *have* no trouble. They *gave* me trouble."

"Can you give me an example of how they picked on you?"

"An example? Hey, I could give you a million examples."

"Give me the last one you remember just before the rape."

"I didn't rape nobody."

"Okay, okay, then the last one before they said you raped the girl."

"Sure. Lemme think. I remember. It was Christmas. Supposed to be a happy time, right? Well, we were having a family party at my mother's house. All my brothers were there with their wives. They was all drinking. But me, I reach for some Dago red and Momma grabs me by the sleeve and says, 'Tony sta d'accord.' That means, 'Take it easy.' They're all guzzling and she don't say shit. I reach for one and she gives me 'sta d'accord.' I'll sta d'accord her. I told her, 'Momma, leave me alone, for Christ's sakes!' But she keeps bugging me, so I really get mad. Man, I started to drink then like it was the last Christmas before they close the Vatican. (Crosses himself quickly.) I got stoned for Jesus, Mary, *and* Joseph. Before I was finished, I broke up a table and two chairs, gave one brother a fat lip he had for two weeks, and I almost broke my kid brother's jaw."

"I guess you did have plenty of trouble. Well, look, I'm going to have to go now, but I'd like to leave you with something to think about. We have group therapy here. Some of the patients and I get together three times a week and sit down to talk over their problems. Many of them have had trouble with their families, too. So whether it turns out that you raped that girl or not, it may help you. You take your time and decide, and I'll come back to talk with you again."

"Hey, Doc, I don't have to think it over. I didn't rape nobody, but if it'll get me a parole I'd join the Communist Party. You count me in."

"Okay. I'll have your name put on the list for group, and you'll begin Monday. But there is no guarantee that being in group will get you out any sooner."

As I left I realized that Tony had talked with a good deal of strong feeling and had gestured dramatically in his Italian way, but he never did get up. He never even righted his chair from its angle of indifference against the cell wall.

From that first meeting, I was sharply aware of the

differences in the cultures that had spawned us. I was certainly responding to something more basic than our contrasting means of expressing ourselves. And yet the differences in our gestures seemed to hold the key to our widely different heritages and the ways in which we learned to see our relation to the world.

Tony's gestures were clearly Sicilian. Though he had never been any closer to his parents' Italian island home than I had been to the Eastern European immigrant ghetto in which my own grandparents were raised, we each could have passed as a native—at least in pantomime. Tony's expansive gestures went out in large sweeping spheres from his muscular shoulders to his hard olive hands. They caught up his audience with the flowing intensity of emotion with which his arms reached upward and outward into the world. The power of his throaty voice was displayed to advantage and dramatized by the crescendo and diminuendo of primitive feelings silently acted out in the smooth strong movement of his arms. He met the world with a passion and gusto, with strong impulse, hot blood, and sudden explosiveness.

In contrast, there was much of the Jew about me. I, too, gesticulated as I spoke, but with none of the Italian pictorial display of feelings. Rather my movements reflected the inner uncertainties and complexities of the obsessive criss-crossing lines of thought that lay behind what I was trying to say. Though I had not myself studied the Talmud, the workings of my mind proceeded in the traditional weighings of alternatives, the delight in communicating and arguing the uncertainties of the inner world, in which the answers kept changing, and in which only the questions were eternal.

The directness of Tony's gestures made it seem that life was clearer and more comprehensible for him. My own non-verbal manner of address was narrower, more confined and irregular. It made itself felt in the shrug of one shoulder, an awry tilt of the head, and the abrupt and intricate movement of my less muscular forearms and almost delicate hands. It was almost as though my

upper arms were attached tightly to the sides of my
body, with all movements confined to extensions from
the elbow and wrist, intricate designs accenting the
complexity of my ruminations. My gestures reflected
the struggle of reason, attempting to emerge from the
tortured trail of blind alleys in an ideational labyrinth.
These were my counterparts of Tony's way of unleash-
ing and pouring forth of lusty feelings.

Yet and still, there was a reciprocity. Each of us
was a man, complete in his own way. Tony was no more
without thought than I was without feeling. It was
more a matter of primacy, one acting out his impulses
and then worrying through the consequences, the other
struggling with the implications and significance of his
acts before being able to execute them. In the course
of therapy, I would be working hard at helping Tony
to understand his feelings as a way of being able to meet
the world less irrationally. And, perhaps if I were fortunate, some of Tony's lustiness would rub off on his
teacher to free me from understanding too well to be
able to express feelings, untrammeled by reason.

The attitude of uncaring resistance, which I saw
in Tony on that first day, continued on into the group
meetings. But after three months of fighting with me
and with the group, Tony's long overdue beginning
was about to occur. This was to be Tony's session.
Perhaps I should have recognized what was coming
when I saw Tony pacing the tier just before the hour
began. I didn't see it coming, but the group did, and
that made it easier for me to play my part.

The focus was on Tony from before the beginning. In various attitudes ranging from listless un-
caringness to tense anticipation, seven patients, all sex
offenders, sat on the facing chairs. The eighth man,
Tony, sweating through his T-shirt, paced around,
swearing furiously. I was admitted to the cell block and
began my long, self-conscious walk down the corridor
toward the seated men. Tony spotted me, stopped pacing, and assumed an air of exaggerated nonchalance.

He spoke as if to the group, but intentionally loud enough for me to hear, "Well, well, like it's the man of the hour." He went on standing defiantly until I was seated. Then, finding only apathy or annoyance on the faces of the other men, he sat down with a great show of casualness.

Martin answered, "You know, Tony, you've only been in therapy a couple of months. I've been in for almost a year, and it's been my observation that when a patient attempts to assume an attitude of . . ."

Ed interrupted, "If you're going to tell him something, for Christ's sake, say it so we can all understand."

"Oh, okay. Sorry," Martin apologized. "What I mean is, when a patient pretends not to be serious in group, he usually has something important on his mind that he's too frightened to mention."

Tony challenged him at once. "You saying I'm chicken. Look, maybe I didn't go to college like you, but I'm a damm man. I didn't fool with no eight-year-old kid, and I'm not scared of nothing."

Ross interceded, "I didn't go to college either, but it doesn't bug me that Martin did. How come you talk about that when he's trying to tell you about . . ."

But Tony didn't let him finish. "Awright, awright, forget about college. Just remember I'm as much of a man as any guy in this building."

Charlie broke in at that point, "Maybe you are. I used to think I was, too, until I got wise to myself. But you should be more respectful to the Doc. He wants to help."

Tony was beginning to be surer of his ground. "Sure, he'll help. What's he know about how we came up? Prob'ly he was some rich kid, never had a fight or nothing. Everybody doing for him. His family fussing over him like he was something special."

I asked softly, "Didn't your family ever make you feel like something special, Tony?"

"Yeah, special," Tony threw back with sarcasm and

disgust. "Like I was so special I was the only one who didn't belong in the family. If I didn't look so much like the old man, I'd . . . ah, can it."

Earl picked it up at that point. "You'd what? You don't have to tell me." Tony began to rise menacingly. Earl stopped him with, "Don't blow up. Let me tell you about me. You weren't in the group yet when I was fighting the Doc 'cause he knew I was a bastard. Yeah, I *was* one. You just got treated like one. I don't even know who my father was. There were so many guys my mother shacked up with. I made out it wasn't true, so scared sombody'd find out. So I was mad at everybody. Man, when I stopped being so mad at the group long enough, I found out . . . (his voice begins to crack here but he goes on). I found out they liked me no matter what. Being a bastard, exposing myself to women, it just didn't matter. I stopped being mad and started to bawl like a little kid. I was ashamed at first, but they made me see sometimes it takes more of a man to admit he needs to cry. Why don't you try it?"

Tony was far from ready to buy all that. "Why don't you just shove it. I ain't cried since I was two years old. Not even when the old man whipped my ass. And he was bull, like from the old country."

With a sense of longing, Don spoke up. "Gee, you had something and you threw it away. If my father only had whipped me just once, so I'd aknown he cared what became of me."

Jimmy, who had been silent longer than usual, countered with, "Crap! My old man was always drunk. He just beat me 'cause I was around. My brother was smart. He got out first. And after a while I stopped being around, too. Hey, Doc, we supposed to settle for that? The old man ignores me when he's sober and kicks the shit out of me when he's drunk. And I'm supposed to take that for love, like Don says?"

I answered sympathetically, "It's hard to settle for so little."

But Jimmy wasn't having it. "Settle, hell, I coulda

done without that S.O.B. quite nicely. Thank you very much, but I'll sit this one out."

I tried again, "Yet you've told us you can't understand it, but somehow you usually get your homosexual lovers to beat you up."

Ross saw the point. "Yeah! How about that!"

Martin explained with usual unfeeling erudition, "I think it's a masochistic compulsion."

Tony picked Martin as his target this time. "I think you're a load of whale shit, college man."

But Jimmy had gotten caught up by my last remark. "No wait . . . wait man. You mean I'm still trying to get the only kind of attention my old man showed me."

Norman broke in ingenously, "That's silly, nobody wants to get hurt."

Martin attempted to reinstate his prestige by explaining to Norman, "Norman, you just never seem to understand. Motives are complicated. They . . ."

But Ross wasn't sitting still for that. "Okay, Martin. No fair lecturing Norman just 'cause he's so used to talking to kids that he's the only one'll let you play the professor."

Norman was only too ready to defend Martin. "I like Martin, Ross. He's very smart. He told me all about astronomy and the planets and everything."

Tony broke in sarcastically, "Somebody ought to tell that guy about life here on earth." The group laughed, but Norman seemed not to notice.

Norman acted as if he'd never heard about all this before. "Didn't you like your family, Tony?"

Tony answered without anger this time. "Like them? Sure, I liked them. I had a good family. Italians stick together. Four brothers. We all grew up in a tough neighborhood. Hey, they used to say, 'Here comes the four horsemen.' We all got in a little trouble, but I kept gettin' into more and more. None of them ever got locked up, except maybe overnight for drinkin' or somethin'!"

I spoke slowly and deliberately, "You're beginning to wonder if it was something about you."

But Tony was wise to me. "Sure, you're just like the old lady. Something wrong, so it must be me."

Jimmy tried to stop him. "He's not blaming you, man. He's just trying to find out what went wrong."

It made Tony sick. "That's it. Stick up for him. What the Hell's the matter with you? He can afford to be generous. He goes home at night. But you, you're stuck here like me, . . . unless we become good boys. Take it and shove it, man."

I moved in, surer of my ground now. "Seems like you feel everybody's got it in for you here, just like at home, Tony."

Ross razzed. "What's the matter, Tony? You want Martin to tell you you got a persecution complex?"

Tony threw it back in his face, "You just can it, or I'll take you outside and complex it up your ass." Everybody laughed, Ross very nervously.

Earl tried to get back on serious ground. "No shit, man, I used to think the Doc was picking on me all the time. He made me see I had a chip on my shoulder. If you are looking for a fight, I guess you can always find it."

Tony spat out defiantly, "I can find it and I can finish it."

"Did you win the fight with your family, Tony?" I challenged.

Jimmy jumped on the bandwagon, "Yeah, how come if you won, you're the one what's locked up?"

Tony seemed less sure of himself as he answered, "Well, I went where I wanted to and I didn't come home till I was ready. And if I wanted to get stoned, I did that, too."

I spoke without waiting, "Did you ever get them to love you, Tony?" A long pause followed during which the group was deadly silent—waiting.

Tony's voice was shaky now, "Get off that shit. They coulda loved me when I was a kid, if they wanted to."

It was Charlie who answered, "Don't make any difference if they don't love you now? I notice you look for the old lady's letters even when she don't send you anything."

Tony was getting desperate now, "Look, stop bugging me."

Ross spoke to the others with obvious weariness, "I'm sick and tired of this. We knock ourselves out trying to help this guy and all he does is tell us to go screw ourselves."

Jimmy was still sympathetic. "Man, he's just unhappy."

But Ross was not to be put off. "Well, so am I. I want to get something out of this group instead of listening to all his tough bullshit. No wonder his brothers got fed up with him."

Now Tony had had enough. He jumped up, fists doubled. "You want to find out if it's bullshit. Okay, okay, I couldn't talk to my brothers, either. I'm through talking, and I'm through with you stoneheads and your group, and with that fat-assed preacher of a doctor. But before I go I'm gonna kick the living shit out of you. They can lock me up in seclusion for a year but only because I'm too much of a man for this group. All you guys always picking on me all the time. Well, I'm gonna pick on one of you for a change. You're a big man with words, Ross. Let's see how big you really are. Get up, you dirty bastard!"

Tony passed my chair, moving fast in a fighter's crouch, heading for Ross who was on the edge of his chair, but still seated. I reached out and put my hand on Tony's arm as if to stop him.

I said softly, "Tony, sta d'accord."

Tony stopped, his movement aborted as if a movie camera, which had projected the image, had ceased to turn. The color drained from his face. As he turned to face me his voice came out in hoarse gasps as though he had just been hit in the pit of his stomach.

"Jeez. For a minute it was just like Momma was here."

There was a long silence. The group looked puzzled

but expectant; they knew this was going to be Tony's session.

He turned to the group, "You know, the Doc, he ain't even Italian." Then haltingly he went on, "When I first come here, I tell him these Italian words, and he remembers. Even says it like a Guinea."

"What does it mean, Tony?" Jimmy asked gently, as if afraid to break the spell.

"Huh? Oh, it means 'take it easy.' My mother used to say it to me . . . but not to my brothers. But, the Doc, I think he just didn't want me to get into trouble."

I looked directly into Tony's eyes. "That's right, Tony, and maybe I'm not the only one."

It made sense to Ross, too, and he wanted to help now. "If you're not still mad at me, maybe the Doc's saying your mother cared about you, too."

Tony began in anger but he could not maintain it. "Oh, yeah! Well you just. . . . Shit, I guess I'm not really mad at you, Ross."

Don spoke with embarrassment, "Maybe we all care about you, but it's hard for one guy to say it to another."

Tony's voice broke completely as he wailed, "Mary, Mother of God." He began to sob, despite his efforts to hold his feelings back. "But they couldn'ta cared," he protested. "They was always ashamed of me."

Tommy was gentle, "Like, I don't mean to get you salty again, but like maybe you gave them reason to be ashamed. I bet you was just like me, all the time playing hookey, stealing things, getting into fights, hollering at your folks and getting stewed."

"Yeah," Tony drawled shamefacedly, "I guess it was me was no damned good, not them."

"You can't have been all that bad if they kept on caring, no matter how much trouble you got into," I said reassuringly.

"Okay, so okay," Tony was crying openly now, "But get off my back, please, please. I can't take it. It's too hard. It hurts too much."

By this time I found that I too was crying, down deep inside. It was the first time I had felt that way in my work. For a long time afterward the feeling reverberated more and more intensely within me, "My God, inside I'm crying too, some for him, and some for me."

It wasn't all gravy after that with Tony. There were many setbacks, but slowly, unevenly, good and warm things began to happen. After many months even the rape was remembered, but less as a sexual assault than as Tony's crazy way of getting his share, and maybe somebody else's share too, whether the girl wanted to give it to him or not. And how much more sobbing and sadness as he learned that the share he really wanted was his for the asking—and always had been!

Part Four: If You Meet the Buddha on the Road, Kill Him!

1. Learning to Learn

No plain not followed by a slope.
No going not followed by a return.
He who remains persevering in danger
Is without blame.
Do not complain about this truth;
Enjoy the good fortune you still possess.[1]
                                    I Ching

Whether pilgrim or wayfarer, while seeking to be taught the Truth (or something), the disciple learns only that there is nothing that anyone else can teach him. He learns, once he is willing to give up being taught, that he already knows how to live, that it is implied in his own tale. *The secret is that there is no secret.*

Everything is just what it seems to be. This is it! There are no hidden meanings. Before he is enlightened, a man gets up each morning to spend the day tending his fields, returns home to eat his supper, goes to bed, makes love to his woman, and falls asleep. But once he has attained enlightenment, then a man gets up each morning to spend the day tending his fields, returns home to eat his supper, goes to bed, makes love to his woman, and falls asleep.

The Zen way to see the truth is *through your every-day eyes.*[2] It is only the heartless questioning of life-as-it-is that ties a man in knots. A man does not need an answer in order to find peace. He needs only to surrender to his existence, to cease the needless, empty questioning. The secret of enlightenment is *when you are hungry, eat; and when you are tired, sleep.*

The Zen Master warns: "If you meet the Buddha on the road, kill him!" This admonition points up that no meaning that comes from outside of ourselves is real. The Buddhahood of each of us has already been obtained. We need only recognize it. Philosophy, religion, patriotism, all are empty idols. The only meaning in our lives is what we each bring to them. Killing the Buddha on the road means destroying the hope that anything outside of ourselves can be our master. No one is any bigger than anyone else. There are no mothers or fathers for grown-ups, only sisters and brothers.

Once a patient realizes that he has no disease, and so can never be cured, he might as well terminate his treatment. He may have been put in touch with good things in himself, and may even still be benefiting from the relationship with the therapist, but once he realizes that he can continue as a disciple in psychotherapy forever, only then can he see the absurdity of remaining a patient, only then does he feel free to leave. We must each give up the master, without giving up the search. If no one is really any bigger than anyone else, to whom then can a man turn? If we are each equally weak and equally strong, as good and as bad as one another, then what is left to us? We must learn that each of our lives can itself become a spiritual pilgrimage, an exiled searching without end. Our only comfort on this lonely journey is that for each man it is the same.

But if there is nothing to be gained, and nothing to be lost, why search? Why go on trying? The Yaqui Indian *brujo*[3] that medicine man, sorcerer, and shaman who is a Man of Knowledge, teaches that knowledge is not something to be finally had, to be kept in a man's pocket. "To be a man of knowledge has no permanence."[4] Rather, there are natural enemies to be challenged, dangers to which most men succumb, such as the first foe, Fear. If a man overcomes fear, he acquires clarity of mind. But this very achievement of clarity becomes the next opponent to be faced. Once fear has been dispelled, clarity becomes the next enemy by tempting a man to give up ever doubting himself. And so it goes. Each accomplishment, itself, becomes the next obstacle to be overcome.

The learning experiences through which a man may challenge such enemies are many. When his apprentice wants to know which route he should choose, the Yaqui brujo answers:" . . . any path is only a path. . . . All paths are the same: they [all] lead nowhere." The only important question you must ask is: "Does this path have a heart?"[5] If it has heart for you, then dare to follow it.

It is important to give up on irrelevant questioning, to take care not to waste yourself. Whenever the brujo's apprentice would ask for explanations or try to reason his way to knowledge, his teacher would turn him round, unhooking him from his head so that he might tumble into wisdom. At one point the brujo turns the would-be disciple on to the "little smoke" (the hallucinogenic magic mushrooms), and teaches him how to change himself into a crow so that he might fly into the sky and broaden his vision. Later the young man asks: "Did I really become a crow? I mean would anyone seeing me have thought I was an ordinary crow?" In essence, the teacher tells him that no proper crow would ask such a question. "Such questions make no sense. . . . Maybe if you were not so afraid of becoming mad, or of losing your body, you would understand this marvelous secret. But perhaps you must wait until you lose your fear to understand what I mean."[6]

But some men never lose their fear. Instead they succumb to it and try to give up the search. Such a withdrawal is not an uncommon phase of apprenticeship, a phase that may even last all the rest of a man's life.

And the brujo-sorcerer himself is never fully beyond his own follies. But he has learned to act with *controlled folly*. His acts are sincere, but they are "only the acts of an actor."[7] Once he has learned to *see* without trying to control his vision with judgmental thoughts, he comes to know that all things are the same. In a sense, nothing really matters, in and of itself, because the importance of things lies in the ways you have learned to think about them.

The Man of Knowledge has come to see that any efforts on his part to try to control the nature of things, or to change others, is useless. At that point he is free to continue to insist on trying, so long as he does not fool himself about the uselessness of his acts. He must proceed *as if* he didn't know. That is the controlled folly of the sorcerer. It is much like the Buddhist's living a natural life, free from the passion of changing that which cannot be changed, but doing what he feels like doing nonetheless, in the absence of illusion. He reaches the point where "whether his acts were good or bad, or worked or didn't, is in no way part of his concern."[8]

Seeing through the eyes of a Man of Knowledge results in our finding ourselves alone in a world filled with folly. That too must be surrendered to. Otherwise, we continue to force meaning onto things, mistaking explanation for understanding. In learning to *see* in this unforced, non-judgmental way, we need not entirely forsake the ordinary ways of *looking* at the world, "because only when we look at things can we catch the funny edge of the world. On the other hand, when our eyes *see,* everything is so equal that nothing is funny." Controlled folly allows us to *look* at the world sometimes, so that we may laugh. Or it may make us cry. It is all the same, except that laughing makes your body feel better than crying does. That is one of the reasons why a man should pick a path with heart, so that he can find his laughter.

So it is that there is nothing to be taught, but yet there is something to be learned. There is something we may come to understand, but not if we demand that it be explained to us. There is something that may happen to us, but not if we await its coming from outside of ourselves.

A man's relation to his own spiritual completion is

movingly described by Martin Buber in his *dream of the double-cry:*

> the dream of the double-cry . . . begins . . . always with something extraordinary happening to me . . . [such as] a small animal resembling a lion-cub . . . tearing the flesh from my arm and being forced only with an effort to loose its hold. [The] . . . first part of the dream story . . . unrolls at a furious pace as though it did not matter. Then suddenly the pace abates: I stand there and cry out. . . . The cry I utter varies in accordance with what preceded it, and is sometimes joyful, sometimes fearful, sometimes even filled both with pain and with triumph . . . in my morning recollection. . . . Each time it is the same cry, inarticulate but in strict rhythm, rising and falling, swelling to a fullness which my throat could not endure . . . a cry that is a song. When it ends my heart stops beating. But then, somewhere, far away, another cry moves towards me, another, which is the same, the same cry uttered or sung by another voice. Yet it is not the same cry, certainly no "echo" of my cry but rather its true rejoinder, tone for tone not repeating mine, not even in a weakened form, but corresponding to mine, answering its tones—so much so, that mine, which at first had to my own ear no sound of questioning at all, now appears as questions, as a long series of questions, which now all receive a response. The response is no more capable of interpretation than the question. And yet the cries that meet the one cry that is the same do not seem to be the same as one another. Each time the voice is new. But now, as the reply ends, in the first moment after its dying fall, a certitude, a true dream certitude comes me to that *now it has happened.* Nothing more. Just this, and in this way—*now it has happened.*[10]

Buber had this dream again and again for years in just this way. And then one night it came again:

> At first it was as usual [it was the dream with the animal], my cry died away, again my heart stood still. But

then there was quiet. There came no answering call. I listened, I heard no sound. For I *awaited* the response for the first time; hitherto it had always surprised me, as though I had never heard it before. *Awaited, it failed to come.* But now, something happened with me. . . . I exposed myself to the distance, open to all sensation and perception. And then, not from a distance but from the air round about me, noiselessly, came the answer. Really it did not come; it was there. It had been there—so I may explain it—even before my cry: there it was, and now, when I laid myself open to it, it let itself be received by me. . . . I heard it . . . "with every pore of my body." [It] . . . corresponded to and answered my cry. It . . . [meant so much more than] the earlier rejoinder . . . in the fact that it was already there. When I had reached the end of receiving it, I felt again that certainty, pealing out more than ever, that *now it has happened.*[11]

Enlightenment and the freedom it brings are always imminent but our very efforts to catch hold of what we are seeking may prevent us from discovering what is already there. There is the image of the man who imagines himself to be a prisoner in a cell.[12] He stands at one end of this small, dark, barren room, on his toes, with arms stretched upward, hands grasping for support onto a small, barred window, the room's only apparent source of light. If he holds on tight, straining toward the window, turning his head just so, he can see a bit of bright sunlight barely visible between the uppermost bars. This light is his only hope. He will not risk losing it. And so he continues to strain toward that bit of light, holding tightly to the bars. So committed is his effort not to lose sight of that glimmer of life-giving light, that it never occurs to him to let go and explore the darkness of the rest of the cell. So it is that he never discovers that the door at the other end of the cell is open, that he is free. He has always been free to walk out into the brightness of the day, if only he would let go.

On our pilgrimage, we are defeated not only by the narrowness of our perspective, and our fear of the darkness, but by our excuses as well. How often we make circumstances our prison, and other people our jailers. If only I were not married or if at least my wife were not so cautious, what great ventures I could pursue. Translation: It's a good thing my wife takes responsibility for reminding me of the hazards of some undertakings; otherwise I might plunge headlong into the abyss. In this way, I can act with realistic caution, while maintaining the image of myself as the undaunted adventurer. But, too, in this way I sometimes forgo recognizing the extent of my freedom, timidly avoid some situations that frighten me, and make excuses for my constraint.

At my best, I take full responsibility for what I do and for what I choose not to do. I see that there is no prison except that which I construct to protect myself from feeling my pain, from risking my losses. It is so hard to hold on to the understanding that ultimately it does not matter what I do. Whatever I gain will not change my life, and whatever pain I may have to endure, I will be able to survive.

Shlomo, an old Hasid . . . exclaimed one day in despair: "What have I gained by becoming blind, since I continue to see myself?" Poor man! He wouldn't have gained anything had he stopped seeing himself. *The game is rigged; there is nothing to gain. And nothing to lose, which makes it worse.*[13]

As we must all soon die, in a way nothing matters. We might as well do what we can to bring our own meaning to our lives. Freedom is just another word for nothing left to lose.

I do not mean to imply by this that a man can determine just what his world or his life will be like. A man, after all, is only a man. He stands somewhere between absolute freedom on the one hand, and total helplessness on the other. All of his important decisions must be made on the basis of insufficient data. It is enough if a man accepts his freedom, takes his best shot, does what he can, faces the consequences of his acts, and makes no excuses. It may not be fair that a man gets to have total responsibility for his own life without total control over it, but it seems to me that for good or for bad, that's just the way it is.

This dilemma of living a life of total responsibility, within an existence of only partial knowledge and partial freedom, reflects the suffering of "Mankind drowning in the Great Sea of Birth, Death and Sorrow."[14] A man who lives in a world without appeal, a world in which God has died, has no one else to forgive him. He will be "punished by his sins, not for them."[15] And so, each day he must forgive himself, again and again. He is subject to his own personal limitations, in a changing world, designed by a lunatic. Each man is capable of warmth, of loving, of understanding, of extending himself, of being transparent and vulnerable to another. At the same time, and *perhaps in the same proportion,* he is capable of evil, sham, fraud, and destructiveness, of closing out the other and wantonly using him.

It does not seem to me that things can ever be improved. New solutions breed new problems, and man is not the perfectible creature assumed by his technology. A man can strive to grow, but this pilgrimage is merely an "unceasing journey from what we seem to be to what we are."[16] Each day, each situation brings with it new uncertainties with which to cope. The world is essentially arbitrary in its movement, predictable only in the least important ways. Yet in each moment of limited understanding and insufficient data, a man must make decisions just as though he knew what he was doing.

Ironically, as a man grows and gains new freedom, he becomes aware that at each point at which he must risk himself anew, aided by his new-found freedom, new experiences for which he is unprepared then present themselves. He confronts new aspects of himself, which, though wonderful, may also be terrible (like becoming a grown-up). The growing edge eats away at itself, and in a sense we have come no further than we were when we first started out. And yet, to be a man, in the best sense, is to be willing to keep moving, though we make no measurable gain. Like Sisyphus, we are destined to forever roll a heavy stone up the side of a mountain, knowing that when we get it to the top, the stone will roll back down again. Yet, "The struggle itself toward the heights is enough to fill a man's heart. One must imagine Sisyphus happy."[17]

This struggle need not, of course, take place in geographical space and historical time. *The most important struggles take place within the self.* I remember how moved I felt as I accompanied one young man through his own painful journey through the inner space of his soul.

Raymond came to therapy because of trouble in his marriage. His life was defined by his abstract theoretical analyses on the one hand and his super-practicality on the other. This worked fine in his professional efforts as an engineering-physicist, though even there he was less creative than his considerable intellect promised. In his marriage, it made his emotionally hungry wife climb the walls.

After helping them to unhook from some of the dead-end tactics of their marital impasses, I began to see Raymond about the problems in his own life about which he had become curious. The central pivot of his tale was his struggle to survive since the age of four when his father had abandoned him by dying suddenly and too soon. After that Raymond had received little loving care, and much neglect and abuse. There was no point in crying about this tragedy (or about anything else), "because tears don't solve problems."

He recalled his father more with bitterness than regret. The old man had been a poor German immigrant to this country, a tool-and-die-maker whose aspirations for something better had led him to tie up a good deal of time and effort and money in correspondence courses. Raymond complained that his father had left him little more than unpaid bills and a carton of old books. Yet Raymond had been able to go on to achieve graduate degrees, in the face of substantial practical obstacles.

I was intrigued by the image of this magic carton of old books. They were treatises on the physical sciences. Raymond cried for the first time since he was a very small child, as he came to realize that his father had left him his own dream as a legacy, a dream that the son had made come true.

Slowly, Raymond began to reclaim the soft and painful feelings that go with being a man. Eventually he became obsessed with going back to East Germany, for a visit beyond the Wall to the little town in which his father was born and grew up. If only he could make this pilgrimage, then he would know who he truly was.

It was only with great reluctance that he followed my suggestion to first make the journey as a fantasy trip. But then one day, with tears streaming down his face, he was able to see himself standing in the square of that old German town, walking where his lost father had walked, knowing what sort of life it had been for the man with a dream who had sired him. We were all there, he and I and his own as-yet-unborn son. He was, at last, his father's son. His deadly practicality fell away. At that moment he learned that what he *felt* was what counted in his life. He knew that some day he could make this literal pilgrimage into the past if he wanted to, but that he no longer *had* to go. His truth lay, not in some distant place, but within himself. He had learned that "the Sage arrives without going."[18]

Sometimes life seems like a poorly designed cage within which man has been sentenced to be free. Condemned to this freedom, it is difficult for a man to face the fact that he feels like a misfit in this life, difficult until he discovers the secret that "all men, finally, are misfits."[19] There seems to be no way out of it:

Once, in the Orient, I talked of suicide with a sage whose clear and gentle eyes seemed forever to be gazing at a never-ending sunset. *"Dying is no solution,"* he affirmed. "And living?" I asked. *"Nor living either,"* he conceded. *"But, who tells you there is a solution?"*[20]

2. The Pilgrimage of the Young

> YOUTHFUL FOLLY has success.
> It is not I who seek the young fool;
> The young fool seeks me.
> At the first oracle I inform him.
> If he asks two or three times, it is
>   importunity.
> If he importunes, I give him no
>   information.
> Perseverance furthers.[1]
>
> *I Ching*

I was a Hipster. Had I lived out my adolescence in the Thirties instead of in the Forties, I would have been a Marxist. Were I younger by ten years (by one teen-age generation), I would have been a Beat in the Fifties. Had I been born still later I would have made my youthful pilgrimage as a Hippie in the Sixties, or like my own teen-age sons, as a Freak (or who knows yet what) in the Seventies. Each generation of adolescents makes its own sort of search for meaning. The pilgrimage of the young is individual, though it is committed in concert. In each generation, a few make the pilgrimage in depth, devoting themselves to it, throwing themselves into the adventure of their lives. Many others make it on a part-time basis, drawing power from identification with the mythic folk hero figures whose commitment is more radical. Some abstain completely and might as well have grown up in the age of their parents. The shape and color and sound of the young pilgrims' journey changes from generation to generation, defiantly defining itself against its predecessors. Yet in every generation the unrest, the seeking, the hunger are the same. In the Forties, I was a Hipster, but mostly I was simply a young seeker.

I don't remember choosing the path of my pilgrimage. The call simply seemed to be in the air. I heard it and I answered. Marxism never did seem like a viable alternative. Perhaps it was done in for us by Stalinism, or by the Soviet-Nazi pact. More likely, that just wasn't where it was any more. The older young-communists whom I knew were appealing only in their workers' folk songs and in their proletariat blue denim jeans and work shirts. (The costumes still appeal, though the meaning of the metaphor is more faded than the jeans.) Their evangelical insistence and their predictable rhetoric made talking with them inevitably boring.

What mattered for "us" was to be *hip*. In the main, "us" were the bright but unhappy, out-of-it kids, who neither played ball nor pleased their families. *Hip* was being in the know, cool, street-wise, a sophisticated primitive whose rebellion was aimed, not at saving society, but at escaping from it. I had no idea then that the term "hip" derived from a much earlier phrase "to be on the hip." It was originally a bit of opium-smoking argot. The smoker lies on his hip, off in his inner world. I did not know that at the time, but if I had known, I would not have been troubled by the image.

I could never have guessed that in the Twenties, my parents had been flappers, committed to the short-term hedonism of speak-easies, the Charleston, and "I don't care." I could only see the empty adult conformity which they seemed to have settled for, and I only knew that I wanted out. They were "nice people" who believed their own slogans: "Don't make trouble," "Stick with your own kind," "Hard work and being good leads to happiness." But "nice people" had fomented two World Wars, had allowed the extermination of six million Jews, and had unleashed an Atom Bomb that threatened to destroy us all. Their morality seemed only to be a matter of appearances. Their conventional wisdom seemed an empty hypocrisy, a dead-end road.

Becoming a hipster was a way of seeking another route, saying "no" to them and "yes" to myself. Despairing of finding meaning in the clean, well-lighted, middle-class world of my parents, I turned my search toward the dark, dirty corners of the demimonde. Like my poet heroes, Baudelaire and Rimbaud,[2] I gathered my Flowers of Evil and spent my Season in Hell. As companions along the way on the hipsters' pilgrimage we sought out other aliens, exiles, and unacceptables. I took to hanging out in the jazz-clubs along Swing Street (52nd Street in New York City), becoming a night person, moved not by the hymns and odes of religion and patriotism, but by Be-bop and the Blues. Harlem and Greenwich Village were my other hideouts. In these hip havens, I moved among musicians, gamblers, petty criminals, dope-pushers, homosexuals, hookers, and other hustlers.

I moved among these outcasts, but never became one of them. Whether because it is required in adolescent pilgrimages, or through some simple failure of nerve, I ventured out again and again, only to return periodically to the security of the home against which I was rebelling. Among the colorfully unacceptable denizens of my hip world, the central mythic hero was the Black. Norman Mailer has called the hipster, "The White Negro,"[3] and the image is not without validity.

We middle-class white hipsters callously romanticized the Negro, just as the Marxists had distortedly ennobled the workingman. It goes on and on. Later generations of young pilgrims have cruelly used their own chosen noble savages. The Beats went on the road, glorifying the lot of the homeless without compassion. The Hippies took on voluntary poverty in a way that made a mockery of the hopelessness of those trapped by being born to be poor. The Freaks become mock Indians, ethnics, and farmers, assuming the dramatic color without appreciation of the isolation and hardship.

Being hip became a way of taking on the "sophistication of the wise primitive,"[4] emulating the looseness and sensuality that we ascribed to Negroes. We saw ourselves as alienated, and yet more privileged than those trapped in the square world. We sought release in the orgasm of jazz, in momentary sexual unions, in the unpredictable adventures of the dark streets. There was no purpose. There were no rules. There was only the endless search for *kicks,* for those existential moments of adventure that made us feel alive.

This seeming freedom of the Hipster must be seen within the context of his being *cool.* There is a hidden self-containment in his unwillingness to be upset or thrown off balance by any of the concerns or norms of niceness and normality that bind the "squares." Our impassivity gave us the untested illusion of magical omnipotence. We robbed the squares of their power by making them uneasy while we ourselves remained passive and unruffled. In our own eyes, we were an elite, in the know, *digging* where it was really at.

It seems to me now that we could not have maintained this pose without the psychopharmaceutical support of marijuana and hashish, and of the drug subculture within which we experienced the life-softening quality of these chemicals. Today, everyone knows about *grass,* either as a problem or as a pleasure. Everyone speaks of it, and even parents try using it. But it is only one of the supports available to today's young pilgrim. Mass media images, hallucinogenic drugs, political protests, and the alliance-strengthening message of rock lyrics provide a network of identity-supporting structures.

For hipsters, marijuana was the central staple of our cultist rituals. We could talk of it openly as *pot,* describing ourselves as *vipers* without worrying about squares' becoming wise to our hip argot. Every Negro seemed *with it,* but we patronizingly found the white middle-class world, against which we defined ourselves, totally ignorant of the secular host of our hip communion. The very act of *copping* (of obtaining grass) was itself an elaborate time-consuming adventure into the neighborhoods our parents had warned us against, dealing with people whom they would have liked to pretend didn't exist at all. Copping was a dark and dangerous delight, which ended in a secret ritual of cleaning the shredded leaves of unwanted seeds and twigs (debris that would otherwise pop and burn without adding to the high). Joints were rolled in zig-zag cigarette papers (miraculously made more available by the wartime cigarette shortages).

Finally, we would light up, each of us speculating from the first drag as to whether this would be really *dynamite grass* or if we had been burned, sold some inferior pot, or even been hustled into buying tea, catnip, or oregano. If so, it was shame on us. By the second time the joint was passed around, our impatience would usually lead to decrying our having *copped some shit* that was not doing anything for us. Ignoring the telltale signs of beginning intoxication (the dryness in the mouth, the softening of body tensions, the buzz in the head), we would begin to talk of other pot, in other times and places. The apocryphal stories would get funnier and funnier, until we realized that we were giggling uncontrollably about things that would not have been that funny had we not been high. Between bouts of fitful laughter we would congratulate ourselves on having been hip enough to have found the grooviest, most fracturing grass of all time.

Often at this point, we would begin to engage in those alternating monologues which we mistakenly took to be profound dialogue. Being high would so narrowly focus my attention that some petty detail of how someone held a cigarette or what a piece of jazz was titled would be imbued with cosmic meaning. Suddenly, in this microcosm, I would see all of the hidden secrets of the universe. My companions would seem to corroborate this through our fervidly inarticulate pseudo-communications. "Like wow," I would say, "Man, can you dig this scene?" "Too much." "Like that's what it's all about," someone would reply. At that moment, it seemed that we both saw the same center of things, understood the universal omphalos, and agreed as to its nature.

I remember one night when someone had tape-recorded one of these insight-heavy exchanges. The next day I was excited by the prospect of listening to these profundities at a time when I was not high. The reason for this was that when I smoked, the poetic transparencies of the universe were vivid, but moments later I could no longer remember what these soul-transforming insights had been. We played the tape. It was disappointing gibberish. I expressed the terrible letdown to a fellow-hipster, saying that if any of the insights had meant anything the night before, I certainly could not understand them now. "Of course not," he replied, "if you want to *dig* what they're about, you have to be high."

It was a trap. It led nowhere. One of the reasons that I stopped getting high was that that colorful fog came to seem like the only reality. Living in between highs was too often an empty drag. Many of my fellow-hipsters began to bridge the gap with heroin. Some of them are now dead junkies, overdosed with illusion. I never tried heroin myself, because instinctively I knew that I would have liked it so much that in an instant I would have become the hippest of junkies, lost to myself forever. Since that time, chemically induced pilgrimages have seemed to me to be misleading detours. The way must not be sought by putting ecstasy into my body, but by finding it within my Self. Drugs can give pleasure and being high can be fun but the essence of pilgrimage cannot be found in a vial.

Even so, the hipster's drug trip did save us from immersion in the empty conformity of our ex-flapper parents, and from the robot-like corruption of the party-line Marxists. It gave us time-out so that some of us were able to find new paths as adults. The Beats, the young pilgrims of the Fifties, saw our ways of seeking meaning as empty and destructive. Allen Ginsburg, one of their early spokesmen, summed up his howling anguish in this way:

I saw the best minds of my generation destroyed by
   madness, starving hysterical naked,
dragging themselves through the negro streets at dawn
   looking for an angry fix,
angelheaded hipsters burning for the ancient heavenly
   connection to the starry dynamo in the machinery
   of the night. . . .[5]

Not that the Beat Generation[6] avoided drugs entirely. They simply used them differently. They became
romantic seekers, trying to get past the hipsters' cynicism and detachment by going on the road in an attempt to rediscover a Whitmanesque America, homeless
sexuals in search of a vagabond self. Ironically, their
own commitment to hallucinogenic drugs was imbedded
in an oriental surrender to the universe, to a life without fixed place or identity. Hashish and morning-glory
seeds were imbibed ritualistically while chanting man-
tras. Curiously, their journey to the East was performed
as they roamed westward across America. Their un-
shaven, unbathed, pioneer-like homelessness offended
Established America though it might well have served
to restore its greatness of spirit.

The pilgrimages of youth serve mainly to save the
children. The rest of the country recoils from the challenges to their certainty, from the foolishly ungrateful
wayfaring of the young. Later on, of course, everyone
benefits, but only when the soul-wrenching vividness
of the youthful pilgrimage has grown stale enough to be
made acceptable by the entrepreneurs. Once what the
kids have to teach us has been made milder, less revolutionary, only then do we adults let it yield a
watered-down lesson.

The Hippies of the Sixties, the Flower Children, set
up a Counter-Culture,[7] which challenged the obscene-
ly callous ways in which we live. But the American
Puritan culture could not understand sex without obligation or the pleasures of drugs without penitential
hangovers. To make love, not war, seemed immoral,
just as giving up material evidences of success seemed

a denial of the technology on which we depend to make a man happy. Yet our present questioning of the old life-denying professings of traditional sexual morality, our recognition of the lunacy of Vietnam, and our uneasiness at the stewardship of the Military-Industrial Complex, all are awarenesses that we owe to our Hippie children.

What may we come to learn from the youthful pilgrimage of the Freaks of the Seventies? Acid trips no longer provide cosmic truths. Tripping just adds color to the fun of sensory experience. Politically they seem to be in two places at once. They challenge the system and avoid the draft, but do so in ways that they hope will lead to sympathetic Supreme Court decisions to humanize the law. They try to radicalize their college campuses in hopes of changing how things are run, but too they drop out to go live on communes in loving, decentralizing, anarchist communities. They break with the capitalistic ideal of the sacredness of private property. They steal from those in power wherever they can, euphemizing their hooliganism by calling it political *rip-off*. Yet they are deeply concerned with human rights, and eschew Communistic totalitarianism as much as that of what is laughingly called "The Free World." Their God-term is *alliance*. They hope for a resurgence of unity, a coming together of the underprivileged. They identify with the ethnic blue-collar workers, the hard-hats who beat their brains out. They feel at one with the Indians, the poor Blacks, the Chicanos. They romanticize the Third World, that great powerless mass of humanity who often finds their efforts irrelevant.

The Liberalism on which I once prided myself is decried as crypto-fascist. I love them, and yet they say that I am the enemy. Perhaps they are right. How strange that, knowing this, I still believe that trusting the young is the only hope of each aging generation.

3. My Pilgrimage to the Sea

> Water flows on uninterruptedly and reaches its goal.[1]
> Quiet return, Good fortune.[2]
>
> *I Ching*

At least once in each year of my life, for almost as long as I can remember, it has been necessary for me to return to the sea. The living waters draw me back to their shores again and again. They seem to wish to show me that though they are ever changing, yet they never change. The ocean is both endlessly calm and disruptively turbulent, alternately quieting my own inner turmoil, while yet insistently warning me of the dark powers that lie unquiet beneath the water's surface, and my own.

Inevitably, if I remain open to the tidal rhythms, the sea puts me in touch with the ebb and flow of my own inner area of unrest, my rising struggles and intermittent surrender and release. My romance with the sea helps me to know both the importance of my own singularity, and the meaninglessness of my trivial being.

As the [Hasidic] saying goes, a man must have two pockets into which he can reach at one time or another according to his needs. In his right pocket he must keep the words: "For my sake was the world created." And in his left: "I am dust and ashes."[3]

For many years now, I have undertaken this pilgrimage with my wife, Marjorie, and our three sons. In order to mask the power and the mystery of the venture, we sometimes talk of the trip as if it were only a pleasant summer vacation on Martha's Vineyard, one of Cape Cod's lovely off-shore islands. But secretly we all know (even the children) that the journey to her magic island and to my great surrounding water ritually reconsummates our marriage.

Ever since we first came together, I have been for her an island on which she could be free from the distractions of a soul-devouring world. At the same time, she has provided for me the sea's life-giving depth and nurturance, an eternal female "thereness" through which the forces of nature flow. Her female wisdom is a fulfilling reciprocal, which matches and completes my parameters. As a man I must struggle against nature, carving out a definition, tearing it away from life itself. During our pilgrimage, she becomes the island unto herself, just as I for a time enter and merge with the sea. At such times, it is as if we each complete ourselves. Ironically, we can then offer more to the other, simply because it is no longer required.

The powerful beginning of the pilgrimage is a rite of passage, which masquerades as a four-mile, forty-five-minute ferry crossing of Nantucket Sound from the Cape to Martha's Vineyard. Waiting for the ferry is always difficult, because of the fear that this time maybe it won't arrive. But each time it finally *does* pull in at the dock, and each time we board with the same maiden-voyage excitement. Standing at the rail of the upper deck, I pretend a naturalist's curiosity about the screamingly greedy sea gulls so as to distract myself from worrying about the overcast sky, the threat of weeks of stay-indoors weather. The boat's whistle blasts unexpectedly, always a shade louder than I remember it.

We begin to move out into the channel. I explain to myself that it is the boat that is moving, that it only *seems* as though it is the everyday world of the mainland that is drifting away. In mid-channel there is once more the sense of being suspended in permanent limbo on the angry choppy waters of the Sound. And as if in a recurrent childhood dream, it is at this point that the change begins.

During this suspension from the disappearing mainland, the unvarying gray of the sodden sky begins to break up into a textured crazy-quilt of all the kinds of party-cloudy/partly-sunny meteorological categories into which the skies can be sorted. Time is compressed as the day changes expression more rapidly than I can read it. I can no longer make judgments. I begin to become frightened by the loss of landmarks. And then, without my ever being able to name the moment when it occurs, the sunlight emerges with soothingly penetrating warmth.

All at once I am aware of how brilliantly the water sparkles. The air, once an impenetrable barrier, is now a lens for eyes till now unaware of their myopia. Everything stands out in a brightness and clarity that make the world seem almost theatrical, more real than real. I am sure that I can see as far as I like. I am disappointed to find that, to the stern, the mainland is out of sight. Then I remember. I turn away from the ship's wake, and there before me, out of the water, thrust the green island hills. The exitement and the relief make me cry joyfully again. I am coming home!

The island itself is typical of those formations plowed out ten thousand years ago by the southward movement of the glaciers, having a long central moraine from which the land descends on either side. The terrain is uneven, alternately thrusting up and dipping down in what are called "knobs" and "kettles." Glacier-tossed boulders and stones are scattered about. The natives use these "erratics" to build low stone walls, which separate one man's land from the next. The island is well-wooded, and fringed with beaches. And everywhere, there are the living waters. Not only is Martha's Vineyard bounded by the Sound and by the Atlantic Ocean, but it is spotted with smaller bodies of water.

Brooks abound, and great salt-water, kettle-hole ponds attract me now as they once drew the Indians who lived along their perimeters. The Indians camped on their banks, feeding on the shellfish and other pond life that are still to be found there. I am drawn to the ponds to feel once more a part of this primitive existence. But too, it is the *stillness* of the pond that calls to me. Looking into the mirror of the unmoving waters, I see the reflection of my own face. The quieting water confronts me with an image of myself that does not flatter. The stillness within me, which its calm elicits, provides an escape from the usual frenetic struggle to adorn my image. The mirroring water reflects the true face, the face behind the mask. It is always something of a disappointment. And yet in a way, it's a relief to see myself as less than I might like to be, but yet, for better or for worse, just as I am.

Though I return to the mirroring ponds again and again, I cannot remain at their quiet edge. Always in the background is the hypnotically rhythmic siren-pounding of the great surf beyond the dunes. As in a dream, empty of my own will, I walk like a somnambulist drawn helplessly back to the Great South Beach. It is on these sands that the winter of my life is revealed in lunatic perspective.

Once on the beach, I am totally engaged by this world's simplicity. Endless blue sky, hung with just enough of soft unthreatening clouds to relate it to the earth; its mythic vastness is more than my gaze can take in. This blue, the ocean's changing greens, and the yellow of the sands, these are the colors of time's beginning. The air is clear enough to crisp my vision, and it has a pure sweetness, scented by only the salt-water smell of life. There is no sound, save for the steady breaking of the surf, the whisper of the windblown sand, and the nasal "criii" of the fish-hungry, sky-arcing sea gulls.

The input of sound and sight and smell is so simple that I cry out with the surprise of sudden relief. It is as though all through the rest of my daily life, without my being aware of the noise, someone else's radio, tuned too loud, had been blaring in my ear. Standing on the beach, I only now become aware of the oppressive cacophony, only now that it has been switched off. My mind is emptied, and I am openly transparent once more.

I walk the wild, empty beaches, past dune-grass-tufted, mountainous sand hills, in the shadow of great, crumbling, ocher clay cliffs, along deserts of sandy flatness. I pocket colorful beach pebbles collected as a hedge against the too unmarked openness of sea and sky. The foaming edge of the breakers teases at my feet with playful unpredictability.

I survey the sea. My vision defines the world. I am the master. Then, perhaps through God's eye, I look in on myself, as if high on hashish. The ocean's vastness is beyond belief. I see myself as a pitiful speck at the edge of a cosmic puddle, a miniscule moment deluding himself that he is in charge of Eternity. It is terrible to be so helplessly alone. Longing burns in my aching chest, my eyes mist over.

At the edge of the sea, I am the last human being left. And too, I am the first man ever created. It is *my* ocean and *my* sky. I feel the power of my sovereignty. It is heartbreakingly lonely. It is only a moment, this time-out. Yet I cannot bear the awful feeling that it will last forever.

Each year this happens. I know that this experience is coming, without ever quite remembering how much anguish it will bring. Yet this is part of why I return to the sea, to put myself in touch once more with my terrible loneliness, to learn again that I must bear this. To remember that this pain is the same for us all, that it is each man's weakness and his strength.

Last summer came close to being my final pilgrimage to the sea. The winter preceding it I had undergone the tortured ordeal of brain surgery during which I almost died, and after which I was psychotic for a time. I was grateful to have survived, though part of the tumor could not be removed and my future was ominously uncertain. My hearing in one ear was lost. I was left with precarious physical balance that I experience as a loss of grace as I move through the world. And pain had become my unwelcome companion, dogging me with two or three headaches every day. If only I could have one day without the pain, it would be like coming up for a gulp of sweet, fresh air, after having been submerged too long beneath the water's surface.

But that winter and spring, shortly after the operation, it was different. Sure, I felt in some ways like a dilapidated wreck on fugitive status from the terror of the hospital. But more than that I felt I had won because I was still alive, with but a few handicaps to overcome. The crisis called forth in me all of the old crazy "I can handle anything that comes along" attitudes that I learned so long ago when my mother would tell her trembling child: "You're not really frightened. You're brave enough to do anything you want (I want you) to do."

The first thing I did while recuperating at home was to write a paper about my ordeal.[4] I was half-dead, scared to death and what did I do but write a God-damn paper about it. It was a wise reaching-out to tell my story, to get myself together, to announce that Lazarus had arisen. It was also a patently absurd undertaking for a sick man. I had been cut down, and tried to make of my tragedy a challenge. I did not see the dark humor in calling a brain tumor a "growth experience."

I got myself together, thrust myself forward toward life, went back to work (too much and too early), even wrote a book. I was in a manic high, denying my losses, my pains, my fears. Friends and patients, who had been generous in their sharing of my anguish up till then, were relieved and happy. I was no longer the pariah who would remind them of their own vulnerability. In good faith, they applauded my courage, and celebrated my return to life. Only my wife, Marjorie, who had taken care of me and had saved my life, was both wise and loving enough to tug at my sleeve and repeat softly, "Be careful, darling. There's something crazy about what you're into." After a while she was even able to save herself by being openly angry at my being so irresponsibly high.

Then last summer, on my pilgrimage to the sea, I crashed. All the madly denied sorrow and hurt caught up with me as I paused, away from the distraction of my work, vacation-vulnerable once more. The undistorted pond-reflection of my real face and the clarity-bringing simplicity of the seascape, combined to put me in touch with my hidden despair. I felt a depth of helplessness and hopelessness that I had not experienced for more than twenty years, not since I was teen-aged, worthless, and lost.

Fear that the remaining sliver of tumor would begin to grow again left me feeling that, rather than someday simply dying, I was to be killed off. Or, worse yet, I felt the terror that I might not die, that instead I would become paralyzed. What would it be like to be trapped alive, imprisoned for years in a dead body? What if I could do nothing for myself, and if no one else would be there to bother to do for me, except out of burdensome pity?

I felt deeply sorry for myself. It seemed to me that I could not stand being so out of control of my life. My wife was there, with her own pain, and sorely open to mine. She later described it as "the summer we cried on the beach." But I was so into myself, so frightened, so determined to reassert my will and to have my own way that nothing else seemed to matter.

I spent many hours huddled on the empty beach, alone and brooding. Again and again, I decided that this was to be my final meeting with the sea, that I would swim out as far as I could, leaving my painful life, like a bundle of old clothes on the shore. And each time, I chose not to kill myself, explaining to myself that my wife and children needed me, would miss me too much. But it was not out of any sense of fairness to them that I did not drown myself. In my nearness to suicide, I really cared about nothing but escape from my own helplessness and anxiety. Recalling what I was up to, even now I still feel ashamed.

When we left the island to go home, I was still very depressed, unsure as to whether I was fit to help anyone else. It was time for me to get some help. But it was so very hard to face. I was feeling so down that the idea of going back into therapy as a patient once more made me feel like my life had been a fraud and a failure. And yet, if I would not go and ask something for myself, then everything I had tried to offer to my own patients was a lie.

There was an older therapist in town—a man whom I trust. He had supervised my work years ago, during a period when my father was dying. I used to go for supervision and cry every time. He had helped me then, and I hoped he would be able to help me again.

I phoned and told him briefly about my illness, and about how bad I finally realized I was feeling, hoping that he might have time free to see me. I was grateful and deeply moved when he told me he would "make time." The day I went to his office, I felt frightened, but was grimly determined to work things out. I told him my story in a detailed and well-organized account, and stated that I wanted to get to work right away, to get past this depression, to get back on my feet. Though sympathetic to the pain of my ordeal, his wry answer to my impatience was: "How come a big tough guy like you is thrown by a little thing like a brain tumor?"

That lovely bastard turned me round in a way that helped me to laugh at myself for thinking that I should be able to handle anything, without sorrow, rest, or comfort. He put me in touch with my own longings when he pointed out that I had resisted going through with drowning myself, *not* because my family needed me, but because *I needed them*. He said softly: "If you kill yourself, you'll never see your wife or your kids again, never. Think how much you'd miss them."

After much crying, and some raging, I came to begin to accept how sick I'd been. This tumor was no existential challenge. I had been cut down, without reason. I was in some ways helpless, and perhaps still in danger, but I was alive, and could have what I could have if only I would surrender to things as they were.

This summer I have returned to the sea, no longer feeling any temptation to swim out and never return. I enter the water to play at fighting the great torrents. My balance remains impaired and my stamina is limited, but my courage has returned. Soon I go with the power of the surging seas, happily body-surfing, allowing each newly breaking wave to return me to the shore where I belong. I merge with the sea only briefly, knowing that I am from the water but not of it. The sea renews me with its dark powers, but I am I, and She is She. My pilgrimage of repeated return to the sea will not end so long as I live. And now I know that I *shall* live, for as long as is given to me. And should my body be battered even more, then I will live as I can, enjoying what I might, having what joy is available to me, and being what I may to the people whom I love. I must continue my pilgrimage, for it is my only way of remaining open to this vision. It is to this end that I must struggle for the remainder of that pilgrimage that is my life.

Along the way, like everyone else, I must bear my burdens. But I do *not* intend to bear them graciously, nor in silence. I will take my sadness and as I can I will make it sing. In this way when others hear my song, they may resonate and respond out of the depths of their own feelings.

We will call out to each other in the darkness of the Great Forest, so that we may not be lost to one another. Then, like the innocent Forest People,[5] for a moment we will live in a world created by a God so benevolent that, when there is trouble, we will know that He must be asleep. And, like the Hasidim, just when life is heaviest with pain and anguish, that is the time when we will dance and sing together to waken the sleeping God of our own lost hope.

Epilogue

The three Dreams and the Laundry List which make up this Epilogue are epiphanies which have manifested themselves to me along the way of my own pilgrimage. I will tell you my dreams, if you will tell me yours.

Dream One—The Bank Job

My first book, *Guru,* had been written out of the personal unity of experience and understanding, which had grown during my years of immersion in the literature of Judaism and Christianity, of the Orient, and of mythology. In deciding whether or not to undertake the writing of my next book, *If You Meet the Buddha on the Road, Kill Him!* I felt much more on the verge of an uncharted journey. This time I would be writing of spiritual pilgrimages, and to do so I myself would have to be willing to enter unknown territory, searching without knowing where I was headed.

My uneasiness about being unprepared for the journey surfaced during a discussion of *The Canterbury Tales* with my wife, Marjorie. I was considering using tales from this medieval pilgrimage framework as exempla in my new book. My wife's intimate involvement with Chaucer's work put me in touch with how much of if I simply did not understand. The scholarship surrounding the text was prepossessing, bespeaking of the unfamiliar classical sources, literary conventions, and meanings of the period with which I had had no truck.

I felt unprepared, and knew that it would be audacious of me to undertake such a venture without entering into formal study of the materials. Perhaps a return to graduate school would do it, this time in English literature.

That night I went to bed seriously considering scrapping the whole idea of undertaking the writing of such a book as an unrealistic fantasy. But that night came the dream, the prophecy that would decide me. For a long while now I have trusted my dreaming self as wiser than that waking self whose head is cluttered with reason and practicalities, so busy trying to control things that he sometimes forgets that the heart has reasons that reason does not know. When I dream, I never forget to trust myself.

To understand my dream, you need to know two bits of data about my writing. The first is that my readers feel most engaged by my throwaway pieces, the things I write easily, intuitively, just for my own fun. The "Eschatological Laundry List" (with which I conclude this Epilogue) is such a piece, the only thing I've written from which someone chose to make a poster, a piece to live with.

The other bit of information that is relevant is that I wrote another short piece, titled "Easy Choice," a piece that made people so nervous that no one would publish it. After three rejections by editors who were interested but uneasy about the article, I gave up submitting it. Instead I decided to trust myself enough to have it Xeroxed and to take my chances on distributing it on my own.

The dream began with my assembling a crew with whom to pull off a bank job. We were all dressed in black, complete with gloves and turtleneck sweaters. Each was a talented expert in his own field, and we all carried special equipment. It was to be one of those professional heists of the Topkapi genre.

Stealthily we entered a building fraught with alarm systems and electronically controlled passages. Somehow it reminded me at the same time both of some

super high-security intelligence agency and of my old
junior high school building. Expertly we bypassed
each security device, as doors slid open, their controls
yielding to our equipment.

At last, we were in the central chamber. And there,
behind an impermeable plastic shield, stood the bank, a
data bank! Instead of a vault, our object turned out to
be an enormous computer that covered an entire wall,
the mother lode of information, the universal data bank.

One of my expert helpers fed in our questions. The
machine was primed. Now if only we could unlock the
answers. The final security device was an electronically controlled slot, which would only be activated by
inserting a specially treated card. It reminded me of the
security check-point machines at the Chicago Demo-
cratic Convention, the ones people found they could
bypass with ordinary credit cards.

I reached into my pocket and took out the specially
treated card, which I was counting on to unlock the
computer. Deftly I inserted it into the slot. For a moment nothing happened. And then, all at once, the
machine went mad. Relay circuits clicked on, lights
flashed, and heralding trumpets blew. Streams of data
poured forth like a ticker-tape parade. We'd done it.
We'd pulled off the bank job of all time.

I was still holding the magic card when I became
distracted by the unexpectedly smooth glossy feel of
it. It felt like a piece of Xeroxed paper. I looked down
at the card, only to discover that, instead of a specially
treated credit card, I was holding in my hand something that I hadn't even seen in years. It was a Chinese
laundry ticket, the kind my mother told me I must
never lose if I wanted to get back the clean shirts I had
to have.

I woke knowing that I was prepared to mine out the
material that I wanted to use for my new book, if only
I could hold on to those things in me that had allowed
me to so easily produce the lovely laundry list, and
that had given me the daring to reproduce "Easy

Choice" on my own. That morning I decided to go
ahead and write *If You Meet the Buddha on the Road,
Kill Him!*

Dream Two—
Nothing Ever Really Changes[1]

An affectionate letter from an old Workshop friend
led me to soft and pleasing musings about how much
I was looking forward to going to the next AAP Workshop. This time it would be in Atlanta. After some
indecision last year, I had chosen not to go out to the
West Coast meeting after all. The winter preceding that
meeting, I had been through an incredible ordeal of the
pain and terror of brain surgery. Though there are a
number of men and women whom I love, and whom
I have never seen outside of the Workshop, it had
pleased me to stay away. It was not, of course, re-
linquishing being with them that was satisfying, but
rather being able to forgive myself for not going out
there "to work my feelings through," choosing instead
to rest safely, quietly, and without obligation.

Workshop experiences over these many years have
remained consistently worthwhile. And more recently,
thank God, the balance has tipped more and more
from my being so scared about what might happen to
the excitement of looking forward to an experience
that would surely be fun even though sometimes scary.
The Workshop experiences for me have nothing to do
with the theme or with the structure against which the
participants fight, still less with the social aspects of
the meeting. For me the heart of it all is neither struc-
tured nor social, but rather open and personal. The
moving and meeting within the open groups, day after day of getting past the hiding, the turning toward
touching and being touched, for me that is the Workshop, and it was that about which I fantasied that
evening.

I enjoyed my musings without at any point becoming aware of my dread. My bed was warm and comfortable, and sleep came as a deepening of pleasure.

In my dream, I found myself already in Atlanta. The Workshop was a kaleidoscopic whirl of affection and excitement, of old friends and new ones, of crying, and fighting, and of loving. And it was all so very, very good. The best Workshop, the Workshop of all Workshops.

Everyone came to me. I had been away, and had been missed. The dark night of my illness was past and everyone was glad to see me alive, together, and still myself. And I was so very glad that I had survived. I even *looked* beautiful, and everyone was happy at how the weight I had lost became me. And then too, there was my book. (On the evening of the dream, it had not yet been published; I was still sweating out the last few weeks to see how it would be received. Secretly, of course, I wanted an underground success in spite of the critics.) But in the dream it had already been published, and it had turned out to mean everything I dared hope for, and especially to these people whose response meant so much to me.

All at once, everything changed. It was dinner time, and dinner time at a Workshop is for me like dinner time at any of the other sorts of meetings that I have avoided for so many years. All was linen and crystal, metal and porcelain. The free play of the groups had given way to the long, ordered tables, fork on napkin, plate with parsley, knife and spoon and the water to taste till the food came.

The people seated at the table to which I felt assigned were familiar to me but each was stuck at a place between two and facing another across the way. They smiled and waved me welcome, but I felt the old dread. Yet having just before felt so good, on I came, but feeling intrusive despite their ease and cordiality.

With smile, and subtle shift of position, they welcomed me into the ongoing dinner conversation. I tried hard to listen, I really did. But it was just the way it

always was: I simply couldn't understand what they
were saying. It was as if they spoke a foreign language.
I never had learned to understand or to speak the social
talk that everyone else seems to use as a way of getting
along and being friendly.

I couldn't do it as a child, and I can't do it now.
That so very old, so terribly painful shyness was still
there, and it still hurt just as much as it ever had. I was,
of course, tempted to do my number of putting their
whole thing down as superficial and without meaning.
But I knew, as I always know, that the bewilderment
and emptiness is at that moment mine, not theirs.

But this was the wonderful Workshop of Workshops.
This was the Time of my Time. And so it was that
I resisted expressing the sarcasm with which I would
have tried to hurt them for being together somewhere
that I could not be, nor did I stride away as if toward
something important.

Perhaps if I waited, at *such a Workshop,* even this
could be different. Without any pause in their conversation, which I still could not follow, a joint was
passed, and then another. A thousand years ago (it
seems), I had smoked my share, and more than my
share when I could get it. After first tasting grass when
I was fifteen and continuing for a number of years
with many days tumbling softly one into the next without my getting straight, I had stopped smoking, just
stopped. I tried drinking but that just put me out of it
without ever putting me anywhere else.

Since then, when a pipe or a joint comes round, I
simply pass it on, without comment, and without regret.
But this time I smoked in turn because this magic time
would be different. After a bit I was high. It was good
and I was filled with nostalgia, but it didn't do it. Being high had never let me go anywhere along with anyone else. There were moments, but mostly there were
illusions. And even now, I dug it, but I still couldn't
understand a fucking word anyone at the table was
saying. I didn't even know how to tell them I was out
of it.

That was when I finally got to it. This is just the way it was going to be. I could lose fifty pounds and be beautiful. I could write my Book of Books, and have it an underground success. I could even die and be reborn. But no matter what, I would always be as painfully shy and as bewildered by the social talk that brings people together, as shy and as bewildered as I had been since I was a kid. Without knowing what you say to leave without hurting, I pushed back my chair, stood up awkwardly, and silently wandered away.

When I awoke I knew, for the first time again, that nothing ever really changes. The shyness is mine, like it or not. It's the best of me and the worst of me, and only the covering it up, the hiding it, and the running from it is not me. And for better or for worse, all of that that is not me is me, too.

Dream Three—My Next Operation

It was the dream I had been waiting to dream, all the while dreading its coming. Some months earlier I had been through a nightmarish ordeal of brain surgery, a bad trip filled with pain and terror. Some of the horror of my experience had been the not knowing; not knowing how much it would hurt, not knowing whether I would be psychotic afterward, not knowing what the outcome would be.

Now it was over, but yet not really over. The surgeon was not able to remove all of the tumor. Some incapacity and distress remain, but there is a good chance that the tumor will not grow again. But too, there is a chance that it will, a chance that I will have to undergo surgery again. That is one of my possible futures.

As the dream began, I was on my way to the hospital. From the beginning I somehow knew that I was not reliving past surgery, but that I was headed for my *next* operation.

This time I knew which plane to take to Boston, where to find a taxi to take me to the hospital, even which entrance to use. A whirl of familiar impressions followed, of administrative procedures as I signed in, was given a room, and underwent preliminary preparations and diagnostic tests. I knew them all. I'd been through it all before.

Very soon I was again gowned, strapped on a table and wheeled into the ante-room to the surgical theater. I recognized and understood each of the life-supporting medical machines, knew well the whiteness and the bright, unblinking, overhead lights. I'd been there before and so felt strangely at ease.

I greeted the doctors and nurses by name, and each one smiled reassuringly at me in recognition. There was only one change, and that was a happy one. This time the surgery was to be performed by the Chinese neuro-surgical resident who had been the only staff member to meet me where I was after the last operation. Then, I had been bewildered by how exhausted I had been after surgery. His explanation had been comfortingly simple, and had spoken directly to my heart when he said: "It is because you have been around the world six times." Over the past few months I had been deeply into reading ancient Chinese poetry, and so when we smiled in greeting, I felt close to him and safe putting myself into his hands.

Suddenly it was time. They wheeled me through the swinging double doors into the operating theater. I understood what was to follow. I recognized the anesthesiologist as he approached the table. And then it happened. Just as he placed the mask over my face, all at once I knew. The bad trip was to begin again. Again it would be a time of terror. I suddenly understood that though I knew how to get to the hospital, understood the procedures I was to undergo, recognized everyone on the staff, and even felt close to my Chinese surgeon, all of this would change nothing. The knowing would not help. I would awaken again psychotic, bewildered, terrified, and in the horror of pain, with my future hanging in uncertain balance.

It will not matter how well I prepare my head for the experience. The moment will belong to God.

An Eschatological Laundry List:
A Partial Register of the 927 (or was it 928?) Eternal Truths[2]

1. This is it!
2. There are no hidden meanings.
3. You can't get there from here, and besides there's no place else to go.
4. We are all already dying, and we will be dead for a long time.
5. Nothing lasts.
6. There is no way of getting all you want.
7. You can't have anything unless you let go of it.
8. You only get to keep what you give away.
9. There is no particular reason why you lost out on some things.
10. The world is not necessarily just. Being good often does not pay off and there is no compensation for misfortune.
11. You have a responsibility to do your best nonetheless.
12. It is a random universe to which we bring meaning.
13. You don't really control anything.
14. You can't make anyone love you.
15. No one is any stronger or any weaker than anyone else.
16. Everyone is, in his own way, vulnerable.
17. There are no great men.
18. If you have a hero, look again: you have diminished yourself in some way.
19. Everyone lies, cheats, pretends (yes, you too, and most certainly I myself).
20. All evil is potential vitality in need of transformation.
21. All of you is worth something, if you will only own it.
22. Progress is an illusion.
23. Evil can be displaced but never eradicated, as all solutions breed new problems.

24. Yet it is necessary to keep on struggling toward solution.

25. Childhood is a nightmare.

26. But it is so very hard to be an on-your-own, take-care-of-yourself-cause-there-is-no-one-else-to-do-it-for-you grown-up.

27. Each of us is ultimately alone.

28. The most important things, each man must do for himself.

29. Love is not enough, but it sure helps.

30. We have only ourselves, and one another. That may not be much, but that's all there is.

31. How strange, that so often, it all seems worth it.

32. We must live within the ambiguity of partial freedom, partial power, and partial knowledge.

33. All important decisions must be made on the basis of insufficient data.

34. Yet we are responsible for everything we do.

35. No excuses will be accepted.

36. You can run, but you can't hide.

37. It is most important to run out of scapegoats.

38. We must learn the power of living with our helplessness.

39. The only victory lies in surrender to oneself.

40. All of the significant battles are waged within the self.

41. You are free to do whatever you like. You need only face the consequences.

42. What do you know ... for sure ... anyway?

43. Learn to forgive yourself, again and again and again and again. ...

Chapter Notes

Part I
Chapter 1

1. Cary F. Baynes, trans., *The I Ching or Book of Changes* (Princeton, N.J.: Princeton University Press, 1950), p. 16.

2. Abraham Maslow, "Self-Actualization and Beyond," in *Challenges in Humanistic Psychology*, ed. James F. T. Bugental (New York: McGraw-Hill, 1967), p. 282.

3. Robert C. Murphy, Jr., *Psychotherapy Based on Human Longing* (Wallingford, Pa.: Pendle Hill Pamphlets, 1960), p. 3ff.

4. Baynes, p. xxxv.

5. Clae Waltham, arranged from the work of James Legge, *I Ching: The Chinese Book of Changes* (New York: Ace Publishing Corp., An Ace Book, 1969), p. 22.

6. Baynes, p. xxxiv.

7. Lao Tzu, *Tao Tê Ching*, trans. D. C. Lau (Harmondsworth, Middlesex, England: Penguin Books, Ltd., Penguin Classics, 1963), p. 57.

8. Paul Reps, comp., *Zen Flesh, Zen Bones: A Collection of Zen and Pre-Zen Writings* (Garden City, N.Y.: Doubleday & Co., Anchor Books, 1961), p. 62.

9. Hubert Benoit, *The Supreme Doctrine: Psychological Studies in Zen Thought* (New York: The Viking Press, 1959), pp. 153–160.

10 *Ibid.*, p. 160.

11. Samuel Clagget Chew, *The Pilgrimage of Life* (New Haven and London: Yale University Press, 1962), p. 144.

12. *Vanishing Peoples of the Earth*, Foreword by Leonard Carmichael (Washington, D.C.: National Geographic Special Publications Division, 1968), p. 119ff. (italics mine).

13. James Bissett Pratt, *The Pilgrimage of Buddhism and a Buddhist Pilgrimage* (New York: The Macmillan Co., 1928), p. vii.

14. J. J. Jusserand, *English Wayfaring Life in the Middle Ages (XIVth Century)*, trans. Lucy Toulmin Smith (New York; G. P. Putnam's Sons, 1929), p. 341.

15. *Ibid.*, p. 362.

16. Chew, p. 147.

17. Matt. 7:13–14.

18. Lao Tzu, p. 125.

19. Jusserand, p. 367.

20. Richard Wilhelm, trans. with commentary by C. G. Jung, *The Secret of the Golden Flower, A Chinese Book of Life* (New York: Harcourt, Brace and World, Inc., A Harvest Book, A Helen and Kurt Wolff Book, 1962), p. 95.

PART I
Chapter 2

1. Cary F. Baynes, trans., *The I Ching or Book of Changes* (Princeton, N.J.: Princeton University Press, 1950), p. 238.

2. *Ibid.*, p. 221.

3. Sheldon B. Kopp, *Guru: Metaphors from a Psychotherapist* (Palo Alto, Calif.: Science and Behavior Books, Inc., 1971), p. 3.

4. *Ibid.*, p. 5.

5. Idries Shah, *The Way of the Sufi* (New York: E. P. Dutton & Co., Inc., 1970), p. 207ff.

6. Henry M. Pachter, *Paracelsus: Magic into Science* (New York: Henry Schuman, 1951), p. 63.

7. K. Rasmussen, *The Intellectual Culture of the Igulik Eskimos*, Copenhagen, 1929, p. 119. Quoted in I. M. Lewis, *Ecstatic Religion: An Anthropological Study of Spirit Possession and Shamanism* (Harmondsworth, Middlesex, England: Penguin Books, Ltd., A Pelican Original, 1971), p. 37.

8. Kopp. p. 35.

9. *Ibid.*, p. 42.

10. *Ibid.*, p. 39.

11. D. T. Suzuki, *Manual of Zen Buddhism* (New York: Grove Press, 1960), p. 106.

12. *Ibid.*, p. 106ff.

PART 1
Chapter 3

1. Cary F. Baynes, trans., *The I Ching or Book of Changes* (Princeton, N.J.: Princeton University Press, 1950), p. 84.

2. *Ibid.*, p. 7.

3. Eli Wiesel, *The Gates of the Forest*, trans. Frances Frenaye (New York, Chicago, San Francisco: Holt, Rinehart and Winston, 1966), un-numbered pages preceding text.

4. Sam Keen, "Man & Myth: A Conversation with Joseph Campbell," *Psychology Today* 5, no. 2 (July 1971):35.

5. Lionel Trilling, "Authenticity and the Modern Unconscious," *Commentary* 52, no. 3 (September 1971):41.

6. Andre Schwarz-Bart, *The Last of the Just*, trans. Stephen Becker (New York: Bantam Books, 1961).

7. *Ibid.*, p. 5.

8. Sidney Jourard, *Self-Disclosure: An Experimental Analysis of the Transparent Self* (New York, London, Sydney, Toronto: Wiley-Interscience, a division of John Wiley & Sons, Inc., 1971), pp. 108–122.

9. Carl Whitaker, psychiatrist and friend. A personal communication.

10. Jourard, pp. 180ff.

11. *Ibid.*, p. 184.

PART II
Chapter 1

1. A. Heidel, ed. and trans., *The Gilgamesh Epic*, from *The Gilgamesh Epic and Old Testament Parallels* in William H. McNeill and Jean W. Sedlar, eds., *The Origins of Civilization* (New York, London, Toronto: Oxford University Press, 1968), pp. 78–152. In this version, the passages put into Latin by Heidel have been rendered into English with the aid of Professor John Hawthorne of the University of Chicago.

2. *Ibid.*, p. 83.

3. *Ibid.*, p. 84.

4. *Ibid.*, p. 87.

5. H. R. Hays, *The Dangerous Sex: The Myth of Feminine Evil* (New York: G. P. Putnam's Sons, 1964).

6. *The Gilgamesh Epic*, p. 100.

7. *Ibid.*, p. 118.

8. *Ibid.*, p. 119.

9. *Ibid.*, p. 127.

10. *Ibid.*, p. 132.

11. *Ibid.*, p. 141.

12. *Ibid.*, p. 148.

13. Sheldon B. Kopp, *Guru: Metaphors from a Psychotherapist* (Palo Alto, Calif.: Science and Behavior Books, Inc., 1971), p. 153ff.

14. Kenneth Rexroth, *Classics Revisited* (New York: Avon Books, Discus Books, 1969), p. 7.

15. *Ibid.*, p. 6.

PART II
Chapter 2

1. Gen. 3:11.

2. *Ibid.*, 3:12.

3. *Ibid.*, 3:16.

4. *Ibid.*, 2:27.

5. *Ibid.*

6. H. R. Hays, *The Dangerous Sex: The Myth of Feminine Evil* (New York: G. P. Putnam's Sons, 1964), p. 144.

7. Robin Morgan, ed., *Sisterhood Is Powerful: An Anthology of Writings from the Women's Liberation Movement* (New York: Random House, Vintage Books, 1970).

PART II
Chapter 3

1. Hermann Hesse, *Siddhartha* trans. Hilda Rosner (New York: New Directions, A New Directions Paperback, 1951).

2. Quoted in Theodore Ziolkowski, *Hermann Hesse* (New York and London: Columbia University Press, Columbia Essays on Modern Writers, Pamphlet 22, 1966), p. 14.

3. Hesse, p. 6.

4. *Ibid.*, p. 8.

5. *Ibid.*, p. 9.

6. *Ibid.*, p. 15.

7. *Ibid.*, p. 20.

8. *Ibid.*, p. 37.

9. Mark Boulby, *Hermann Hesse: His Mind and Art* (Ithaca and London. Cornell University Press, 1967), p. 136.

10. Hesse, p. 58.

11. *Ibid.*, p. 59.

12. *Ibid.*, p. 68.

13. *Ibid.*, p. 82ff.

14. Sheldon B. Kopp, *Guru: Metaphors from a Psychotherapist* (Palo Alto, Calif.: Science and Behavior Books, Inc., 1971), p. 110.

15. Boulby, p. 144.

16. Hesse, p. 90.

17. *Ibid.*, p. 97.

18. Boulby, p. 147.

19. Hesse, p. 109.

20. *Ibid.*, p. 110.

21. Theodore Ziolkowski, *The Novels of Hermann Hesse: A Study in Theme and Structure* (Princeton, N.J.: Princeton University Press, 1965), p. 176.

22. Boulby, p. 149.

23. Hesse, p. 133.

24. *Ibid.*, p. 144.

25. Boulby, p. 150.

26. Hesse, p. 153.

27. Arthur Waley, *The Way and Its Power: A Study of the Tao Tê Ching and Its Place in Chinese Thought* (New York: Grove Press, Evergreen Edition, 1958), p. 195.

28. *Ibid.*, p. 187.

29. Chuang Tzu, XIII, 1. Quoted in Waley, p. 58 (italics mine).

PART II
Chapter 4

1. Geoffrey Chaucer, *The Canterbury Tales*, trans. Nevill Coghill (Baltimore, Md.: Penguin Books, 1952), p. 17.

2. Marchette Chute, *Geoffrey Chaucer of England* (New York: E. P. Dutton & Co., 1946), p. 204.

3. Nevill Coghill, "The Prologue to *The Canterbury Tales*," in *Chaucer and His Contemporaries: Essays on*

Medieval Literature and Thought, ed. Helaine Newstead (Greenwich, Conn.: Fawcett Publications, Inc., 1968), p. 165.

4. Chaucer, p. 299ff.

5. *Ibid.*, p. 276.

6. *Ibid.*, p. 288.

7. *Ibid.*

8. Charles A. Owen, Jr., "The Crucial Passages in Five of *The Canterbury Tales*," in *Discussions of The Canterbury Tales*, ed. Charles A. Owen, Jr., (Boston, Mass.: D. C. Heath and Co., 1961), p. 84.

9. Chaucer, p. 298.

10. *Ibid.*, ff. (italics mine).

11. *Ibid.*, p. 299.

12. *Ibid.*, p. 302 (italics mine).

13. *Ibid.*

14. *Ibid.*, p. 303.

15. *Ibid.*

16. *Ibid.*, p. 308.

17. Kate Millett, *Sexual Politics* (Garden City, N.Y.: Doubleday & Co., Inc., 1970).

PART II
Chapter 5

1. William Shakespeare, *Macbeth* in *Four Great Tragedies* (New York: Washington Square Press, 1939), pp. 328–393.

2. *Ibid.*, p. 340.

3. *Ibid.*, pp. 332, 336, 340.

4. *Ibid.*, p. 337.

5. *Ibid.*, p. 341.

6. Anaïs Nin, *The Diary of Anaïs Nin, Volume I, 1931–1934*, ed. Gunther Stuhlman (New York: Harcourt, Brace & World, Inc., A Harvest Book, The Swallow Press, 1966), p. 91.

7. Sheldon B. Kopp, *Guru: Metaphors from a Psychotherapist* (Palo Alto, Calif.: Science and Behavior Books, Inc., 1971), p. 154.

PART II
Chapter 6

1. Miguel de Cervantes Saavedra, *Don Quixote (The*

Ingenious Gentleman, Don Quixote de la Mancha), in *The Portable Cervantes*, trans. and ed. Samuel Putnam (New York: Viking Press, 1951), pp. 48–702.

2. *Ibid.*, p. 59.

3. Jose Ortega y Gasset, *Meditations on Don Quixote*, trans. Evelyn Rugg and Diego Marin (New York: W. W. Norton & Co., Inc., 1961), p. 51.

4. Joseph Wood Krutch, *Five Masters: A Study in the Mutations of the Novel* (Bloomington, Ind.: Indiana University Press, A Midland Book, 1959), p. 81.

5. *Ibid.*, p. 98.

6. Cervantes, p. 110.

7. Krutch, p. 78.

8. Sheldon B. Kopp, *Guru: Metaphors from a Psychotherapist* (Palo Alto, Calif.: Science and Behavior Books, Inc., 1971), p. 163ff.

9. Donald D. Lathrop, M.D. Quoted by permission from a personal, unpublished letter.

10. Cervantes, p. 34.

11. Salvador de Madariaga, *Don Quixote: An Introductory Essay in Psychology* (London: Oxford University Press, Oxford Paperbacks, 1961), p. 185.

PART II
Chapter 7

1. Dante Alighieri, *The Inferno*, trans. John Ciardi (New York and Toronto: The New American Library, A Mentor Classic, 1954).

2. Francis Fergusson, *Dante's Dream of the Mind: A Modern Reading of the Purgatorio* (Princeton, N.J.: Princeton University Press, 1953), p. 5.

3. T. S. Eliot, "Dante," in *The Sacred Wood: Essays on Poetry and Criticism* (New York: Barnes and Noble, 1960, and London: Methuen & Co., Ltd., University Paperbacks), p. 170ff.

4. Dante, p. 42.

5. *Ibid.*, p. 43.

6. *Ibid.*, ff.

7. C. G. Jung, *Wirklichkeit der Seele* (Zurich: Ascher, 1934), p. 52. Quoted in *Psychological Reflections: An Anthology of the Writings of C. G. Jung*, ed. Jolande Jacobi

(New York: Harper and Row, Harper Torch-books, The Bollingen Library, 1961), p. 75.

8. Dante, p. 54.

9. *Ibid.*, p. 66.

10. *Ibid.*, p. 161.

11. C. G. Jung, "Versuch einer Darstellung der psycho-analytischen Theorie," *Jahrbuch für psychoanalytische und psychopathologische Forschungen* (Liepzig and Vienna: Deuticke, v 1913), p. 106: Quoted in *Psychological Reflections: An Anthology of the Writings of C. G. Jung,* ed. Jolande Jacobi (New York: Harper and Row, Harper Torch-books, The Bollingen Library, 1961), p. 75.

12. C. G. Jung, "Zur gegenwartigen Lage der Psychotherapie," *Zentralblatt für Psychotherapie und ihre Grenzgebiete,* VII (1934)2. p. 12ff. Quoted in *Psychological Reflections: An Anthology of the Writings of C. G. Jung,* ed. Jolande Jacobi (New York: Harper and Row, Harper Torch-books, The Bollingen Library, 1961), p. 73.

13. Lao Tzu, *Tao Tê Ching* (Harmondsworth, Middlesex, England: Penguin Books, Ltd., Penguin Classics, 1963), p. 123.

PART II
Chapter 8

1. Franz Kafka, *The Castle,* Definitive Edition, trans. Willa and Edwin Muir with additional materials trans. Eithne Wilkins and Ernst Kaiser (New York: The Modern Library, 1969).

2. Thomas S. Szasz, "Psychotherapy: A Socio-Cultural Perspective," invited address presented at the Tenth Annual Conference of the American Academy of Psychotherapists, Washington, D.C., October 16, 1965.

3. Hobart F. Thomas, "Encounter—The Game of No Game," in *Encounter: The Theory and Practice of Encounter Groups,* ed. Arthur Burton (San Francisco: Jossey-Bass, 1969), pp. 69–80.

4. Robert Abbott, *Abbott's New Card Games* (New York: Funk & Wagnalls, 1963).

PART II
Chapter 9

1. Henri A. Talon, *John Bunyan,* Writers and Their

Works, Pamphlet No. 73 (London, New York, Toronto: Longmans, Green and Co., 1965), p. 9.

2. John Bunyan, *Grace Abounding to the Chief of Sinners* (London: SCM Press, Ltd., 1955), p. 12.

3. John Bunyan, *The Pilgrim's Progress*, ed. Roger Sharrock (Baltimore, Md.: Penguin Books, 1965).

4. *Ibid.*, p. 39.

5. *Ibid.*

6. *Ibid.*, p. 41.

7. *Ibid.*, p. 46.

8. *Ibid.*, p. 49.

9. *Ibid.*, p. 53.

10. *Ibid.*, p. 56.

11. Talon, p. 24.

12. Marshall McLuhan, *Understanding Media: The Extensions of Man* (New York, London, Sydney, Toronto: McGraw-Hill Paperbacks, 1965), p. 13.

13. Sheldon B. Kopp, *Guru: Metaphors from a Psychotherapist* (Palo Alto, Calif.: Science and Behavior Books, Inc., 1971), p. 97.

14. McLuhan, p. 7 (italics mine).

15. *Ibid.*, p. 23.

PART II
Chapter 10

1. Joseph Gaer, *The Legend of the Wandering Jew* (New York: The New American Library, A Mentor Book, 1961).

2. *Ibid.*, p. 105.

3. Matt. 16:28.

4. Paul Tillich, *The Courage to Be* (New Haven, Conn.: Yale University Press, 1952), pp. 40–54.

5. Albert Camus, *The Myth of Sisyphus and Other Essays*, trans. Justin O'Brien (New York: Vintage Books, 1959), p. 3.

6. Job 3:20–26.

7. Sheldon B. Kopp, *Guru: Metaphors from a Psychotherapist* (Palo Alto, Calif.: Science and Behavior Books, Inc., 1971), p. 43.

8. Colin M. Turnbull, *The Forest People: A Study of the Pygmies of the Congo* (New York: Simon and Schuster, 1968), p. 93.

PART II
Chapter 11
1. Joseph Conrad, *Heart of Darkness*, in *Heart of Darkness, Almayer's Folly, and The Lagoon* (New York: Dell Publishing Co., The Laurel Conrad Series, 1960).

2. *Ibid.*, p. 70.

3. Quoted in *Bullfinch's Mythology*, a modern abridgment by Edmund Fuller (New York: Dell Publishing Co., A Laurel Classic, 1959), p. 239.

4. Arthur Miller, *After the Fall* (New York: Viking Press, 1964), p. 128.

5. Conrad, p. 116.

PART III
Chapter 2
1. The first section of this tale was originally published under the title "A Mother's Love," in *Voices* 2 no. 1 (Spring 1966):102–103.

PART III
Chapter 3
1. A slightly different version of this tale first appeared in *Voices* 2 no. 4 (Winter 1967):88–94.

PART IV
Chapter 1
1. Cary F. Baynes, trans., *The I Ching or Book of Changes* (Princeton, N.J.: Princeton University Press, Bollingen Series XIX, 1950), p. 50.

2. A basic source book for Zen wisdom is *Zen Flesh, Zen Bones: A Collection of Zen and Pre-Zen Writings*, comp. Paul Reps (Garden City, N.Y.: Doubleday & Co., Anchor Books, 1961).

3. The basic source books of Yaqui wisdom are Carlos Castenada, *The Teachings of Don Juan: A Yaqui Way of Knowledge* and *A Separate Reality: Further Conversations with Don Juan* (New York: Simon and Schuster, 1968 and 1971).

4. Castenada, *The Teachings of Don Juan*, p. 200.

5. *Ibid.*, p. 106.

6. *Ibid.*, p. 183.

7. Castenada, *A Separate Reality*, p. 100.

8. *Ibid.*, p. 107.

9. *Ibid.*, p. 104.

10. Martin Buber, *Between Man and Man,* trans. Ronald Gregor Smith (London: Routledge and Kegan Paul, 1947), pp. 1–3.

11. *Ibid.*

12. Hubert Benoit, *The Supreme Doctrine: Psychological Studies in Zen Thought* (New York: Viking Press, 1955), p. 175.

13. Elie Wiesel, *A Beggar in Jerusalem,* trans. Lily Edelman and Elie Wiesel (New York: Avon Books, 1970), p. 15 (italics mine).

14. Christmas Humphreys, *The Wisdom of Buddhism* (New York and Evanston: Harper and Row, Harper Colophon Books, 1960), p. 36.

15. *Ibid.*, p. 21.

16. *Ibid.*, p. 22.

17. Albert Camus, *The Myth of Sisyphus and other Essays,* trans. Justin O'Brien (New York: Alfred A. Knopf, Vintage Books, 1955), p. 91.

18. Arthur Waley, *The Way and Its Power: A Study of the Tao Tê Ching and Its Place in Chinese Thought* (New York: Grove Press, 1958), p. 100.

19. Melvin Maddock, "A 49-Year-Old With a Future," review of Harding Lemay's *Inside, Looking Out, Life Magazine* April 16, 1971, p. 12.

20. Wiesel, p. 15ff. (italics mine).

PART IV
Chapter 2

1. Cary F. Baynes, trans., *The I Ching or Book of Changes* (Princeton, N.J.: Princeton University Press, Bollingen Series XIX, 1950), pp. 20ff.

2. *Baudelaire, Rimbaud, Verlaine: Selected Verse and Prose Poems,* ed. Joseph M. Bernstein (New York: The Citadel Press, 1947).

3. Norman Mailer, *The White Negro* (San Francisco: City Lights Books, 1970).

4. *Ibid.*

5. Allen Ginsburg, "Howl," in *The New American Poetry* ed. Donald M. Allen (New York: Grove Press and London: Evergreen Books, 1960), p. 182.

6. Bruce Cook, *The Beat Generation* (New York: Charles Scribner's Sons, 1971).

7. Theodore Roszak, *The Making of a Counter Culture: Reflections on the Technocratic Society and Its Youthful Opposition* (Garden City, N.Y.: Doubleday & Co., Anchor Books, 1969).

PART IV
Chapter 3

1. Cary F. Baynes, trans., *The I Ching or Book of Changes* (Princeton, N.J.: Princeton University Press, Bollingen Series XIX, 1950), p. 116.

2. *Ibid.*, p. 99.

3. Sheldon B. Kopp, *Guru: Metaphors from a Psychotherapist* (Palo Alto, Calif.: Science and Behavior Books, Inc., 1971), p. 40.

4. *Ibid.*, Epilogue, pp. 159–166.

5. Colin M. Turnbull, *The Forest People: A Study of the Pygmies of the Congo* (New York: Simon and Schuster, A Clarion Book, 1961), p. 93.

EPILOGUE

1. "Dream Two" originally appeared in *Voices* 8 no. 2 (Fall 1971):48–49.

2. "The Laundry List" originally appeared in *Voices* 6 no. 2 (Fall 1970):29.

Suggested Reading

The Pilgrimage Tales

Alighieri, Dante. *The Inferno*. A verse rendering for the modern reader by John Ciardi, Historical Introduction by Archibald T. McAllister. New York and Toronto: The New American Library, A Mentor Classic, 1954.

Bunyan, John. *The Pilgrim's Progress*. Edited with an Introduction by Roger Sharrock. Baltimore, Md.: Penguin Books, 1965.

Cervantes (Miguel de Cervantes Saavedra). *Don Quixote (The Ingenious Gentleman, Don Quixote de la Mancha)*, in *The Portable Cervantes*. Translated and edited with an Introduction and Notes by Samuel Putnam. New York: The Viking Press, 1951, pp. 48–702.

Chaucer, Geoffrey. *The Canterbury Tales*. Translated into Modern English by Nevill Coghill. Baltimore, Md.: Penguin Books, 1952.

Conrad, Joseph. *Heart of Darkness* in *Heart Of Darkness, Almayer's Folly, The Lagoon: Three Tales by Joseph Conrad*. General Introduction by Albert J. Guerard. New York: Dell Publishing Co., The Laurel Conrad Series, 1960, pp. 25–125.

Genesis. The Holy Bible. Revised Standard Version.

Gaer, Joseph. *The Legend of the Wandering Jew*. New York: The New American Library, A Mentor Book, 1961.

The Gilgamesh Epic, from *The Gilgamesh Epic and Old Testament Parallels*. Edited and translated by A. Heidel. Chicago: Chicago University Press, 1946 and 1949. In *The Origins of Civilization*. Edited by William H. McNeill and Jean W. Sedlar. New York, London, Toronto: Oxford University Press, 1968, pp. 78–152. In this version, the passages put into Latin by Heidel have been rendered into English with the aid of Professor John Hawthorne of the University of Chicago.

Hesse, Herman. *Siddhartha*. Translated by Hilda Rosner. New York: Directions Publishing Corp., A New Directions Paperback, 1951.

Kafka, Franz. *The Castle*. Definitive Edition. Translated from the German by Willa and Edwin Muir with additional materials translated by Eithne Wilkins and Ernst Kaiser, with an Homage by Thomas Mann. New York: The Modern Library, 1969.

Shakespeare, William. *Macbeth* in *Four Great Tragedies* by William Shakespeare. Cambridge Text and Glossaries, complete and unabridged. New York: Washington Square Press, 1939, pp. 328–393.

GUIDES ALONG THE WAY

Camus, Albert. *The Myth of Sisyphus and Other Essays*. Translated from the French by Justin O'Brien. New York: Vintage Books, 1959.

Castenada, Carlos. *The Teachings of Don Juan: A Yaqui Way of Knowledge* (1969) and *A Separate Reality: Further Conversations with Don Juan* (1971). New York: Simon and Schuster.

The I Ching or Book of Changes. The Richard Wilhelm Translation, rendered into English by Cary F. Baynes. Foreword by C. G. Jung, Preface to the Third Edition by Hellmut Wilhelm, Bollingen Series XIX. Princeton, N.J.: Princeton University Press, 1950.

Jung, C. G. *Psychological Reflections: An Anthology of the Writings of C. G. Jung*. Selected and edited by Jolande Jacobi. New York: Harper and Row, 1961. (Original copyright by Bollinger Foundation, Inc., New York, 1953).

Kopp, Sheldon B. *Guru: Metaphors from a Psychotherapist*. Palo Alto, Calif.: Science and Behavior Books, Inc., 1971.

Waley, Arthur. *The Way and Its Power: A Study of the Tao Tê Ching and Its Place in Chinese Thought*. New York: Grove Press, Evergreen Edition, 1958.

ABOUT THE AUTHOR

DR. SHELDON B. KOPP is a psychotherapist and teacher of psychotherapy in Washington, D.C. He received his Ph.D. from the New School for Social Research and for twenty years, in addition to maintaining a private practice, has served on the staffs of prisons, hospitals and clinics. He has published in such publications as *Psychology Today*, *American Journal of Psychotherapy* and *Psychiatric Quarterly*, and is the author of *Guru, The Hanged Man* and *IF YOU MEET THE BUDDHA ON THE ROAD, KILL HIM!*

NEW AGE CLASSICS
ENDURING BOOKS FOR OUR TIME AND BEYOND

☐ 27747 **ZEN AND THE ART OF MOTORCYCLE** $5.50
MAINTENANCE, Robert M. Pirsig

The fabulous journey of a man in search of himself . . .
"Profoundly important . . . intellectual entertainment of
the highest order." —New York Times

☐ 26382 **DANCING WU LI MASTERS: An Overview** $4.95
of the New Physics, Gary Zukov

"The Bible" for those who are curious about the mind-
expanding discoveries of advanced physics, but who have
no scientific background.

☐ 26299-8 **ENTROPY: A New World View,** Jeremy Rifkin $4.50

Tells us why our existing world view is crumbling and
what will replace it.

"An appropriate successor to . . . SILENT SPRING, THE
CLOSING CIRCLE and SMALL IS BEAUTIFUL."
—Minneapolis Tribune

☐ 34584 **THE MIND'S I: Fantasies and Reflections** $13.95
on Self and Soul, Douglas R. Hofstadter
and Daniel C. Dennett

A searching, probing book that delves deeply into the
domain of self and self-consciousness. Co-authored by
the winner of the Pulitzer Prize.

"Invigorating . . . a heavy set of tennis for the brain."
—Village Voice

☐ 34683 **METAMAGICAL THEMAS: Questing for the** $15.95
Essence of Mind and Pattern,
Douglas R. Hofstadter

The national bestseller by the Pulitzer Prize-winning
author of GODEL, ESCHER, BACH.

For your convenience use this page to order.

Shirley MacLaine Times Four!!!

Special Offer
Buy a Bantam Book
for only 50¢.

Now you can have Bantam's catalog filled with hundreds of titles plus take advantage of our unique and exciting bonus book offer. A special offer which gives you the opportunity to purchase a Bantam book for only 50¢. Here's how!

By ordering any five books at the regular price per order, you can also choose any other single book listed (up to a $5.95 value) for just 50¢. Some restrictions do apply, but for further details why not send for Bantam's catalog of titles today!

Just send us your name and address and we will send you a catalog!

BANTAM BOOKS, INC.
P.O. Box 1006, South Holland, Ill. 60473

Mr./Mrs./Ms. _____
(please print)

Address _____

City _____ State _____ Zip _____

FC(A)—10/87

Please allow four to six weeks for delivery.

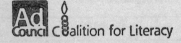
LWA